All About You

An Adopted Child's Memoir

Liz Butler Duren

At fifteen, Liz learns a long-held secret about her life.

She was adopted.

This discovery leads Liz on a 29-year journey to find the mother who gave her away. Like a master detective, she deciphers decades-old agency documents to decode the truths within. Fraught with dead ends and disappointments, her journey threatens to reveal secrets that have long defined the lives of her loved ones. Told with heart, humor and bittersweet reflections of a South Carolina girlhood, *All About You* will resonate with any reader struggling to find their place in the world.

ISBN-13: 978-0-9982794-2-8
ISBN-10: 0-9982794-2-8

Library of Congress Catalog Number Applied For

All About You is a memoir. I have tried to recreate events, locales and conversations from my memories of them. In order to maintain their anonymity in some instances I have changed the names of individuals and places, I may have changed some identifying characteristics and details such as physical properties, occupations and places of residence.

Liz Butler Duren

A FOREWORD

These are things I know to be true about myself.

I was an overly dramatic child. This led to impulsive behaviors and moods that swung back and forth like the rope swing hanging from the live oak tree in my parents' back yard.

This led to me being an overly dramatic teenager and then, without interruption, an overly dramatic woman.

If I were a superhero, I would have been The Exaggerator.

This gift of imagination was the best thing that ever happened to me. It took me on flights of fancy, carrying me beyond the limited imaginations of ordinary people. It allowed me to see the world from different perspectives. It led me on impulsive adventures and made me braver than I actually was.

Sometimes, I think that if I hadn't allowed this part of my personality to take over, I would have had a quieter life with a lot less heartbreak and confusion. I wouldn't have lived in a world where I felt I was the brunt of some cosmic joke being whispered about me behind my back. I could have kept my blinders on and walked through life without asking questions, without wanting my life to be different from what it was.

Something was different, though, and I knew it. I felt it. From the time I was a young girl, this idea crept into my mind that I was not the person everyone told me I was. This idea became the thread of a different color that wove itself into every moment of my life, creating a tapestry stained with a secret.

I could tell you the story about all the adventures of my life, my failures, unrequited loves, two divorces, the jobs I had, the struggles finding myself. I could tell a story about the successes of my life, finally finding the love of my life, having four beautiful and kind children, and the amazing job I love. But no matter what I was doing or how I was feeling, this other story, this idea, was always on my mind and in my heart.

My obsession with it led me to tell this story many times and to anyone who would listen.

I have told it sitting in loud, smoky bars, curled up on a friend's sofa having a late night chat, on sunny beaches with my toes in the sand, at fancy restaurants, and over long-cold cups of coffee.

I never really know how to tell my story. Where do I start? It has been sitting so long with me now that the questions and the answers have become muddled in my mind. It is the melody that I can never quite get out of my head. For so long, I would tell this story with no real answers and no idea of how to get them. So many times the topic has come up in conversation because I was looking for help. What new insights could someone else give me to put me on the right path? So it usually starts at the point where it is the most raw.

I have always wanted to write my story, but I was anxious about reliving it. Not all of it; some of it was quite good, but most of it was hard. I didn't want to be that young, vulnerable girl again. Speaking is easier; I can choose what not to dwell on. The pain can be easily masked or ignored. If I write it, then I need to look at all those emotions. Not just mine but those of the people around me, the ones who loved me that were affected by it.

I asked a friend to write it for me, but he said he couldn't. It had to be my voice.

I spent the better part of a morning in front of my computer with the microphone on. I believed that I could speak it and let the truth flow out of me. Maybe listening to myself would be helpful. I settled into my desk chair with a cup of hot tea in my hands and the silence of the house surrounding me.

I started at what I thought was the beginning and explored the ways it made me feel. I spent several hours feeling the unencumbered emotions and letting them come through uncensored. This was just for me; no one would ever have to hear this if I chose not to share it. I was emotionally drained by the end of the second hour and needed a break. I just wanted to step away from everything for a moment and go for a walk to clear my head and figure out how to move to the next phase of this story. Then I realized that I had never actually started the recording.

After that, words were constantly swimming around in my head, waking me up at night and lingering, preventing sleep's peaceful return. I had opened Pandora's box and I knew if I wanted to expel the demons, I was going to have to let them out. It wasn't going to be easy for anyone to read, myself included, but it was time. I had spent too many years spinning my tale for it to remain in me any longer, torturing me with its memories. At the very least, this was going to be my therapy.

WHO is my birth mother?

WHY did she give me up?

WHERE is she now?

WHAT does she look like?

WILL she be like me?

DOES she think of me?

My journey was a long one. I had no idea in the beginning that it was to be an unbelievable twenty-nine-year venture. It began, as most things do, with an idea, a simple cast off of an idea at first, but the spark it ignited became a constant that never left me.

The friends and lovers in my life are a huge part of this story. They listened to the tale and offered to help. They debated all of the curiosities with me. They encouraged me, discouraged me, offered to go on search parties with me, and begged me not to go.

I remember the day of resolution. The day I finally got what I had always wanted. It was the one step I had to take all by myself. I wasn't used to that. I had depended on the emotional support of so many, and they couldn't take this last step with me. How will I know what to think if they are not there to hash it all out with me? How will I know what to say if they aren't there to coach me? *What will I wear?*

I took a moment, sitting in my car, trying not to cry, to send a quick message to each person that had stood by me and supported me. I told them that I wished I could put them in my pocket and take them with me. Like me, they were waiting for this day and were just as invested. Knowing that they were all waiting with as much anxiety as I was had made the last steps a little easier.

I got out of my car on a hot summer day in my new pink dress, and I knocked on her door.

THE BEGINNING

It all started with a picture.

Family portrait Spring 1978

We had never done a full family picture before. Sure, there were pictures of my big brother, Jonathan, and me, propped up on shag-rug-covered boxes at Grant's Department Store in whatever my mother put us in, usually something itchy. This next portrait would replace the space in the frame that held every 8x10 image from year to year.

My father always carried a smaller copy with him in his wallet. He never replaced the older ones. He just kept them as a small stack tucked neatly away in one of the leather folds.

He would say to me, "Elizabeth, do you want to see a picture of two monkeys?" "YES!" I would reply. The latest picture of us would emerge. I would roll with giggles. This silly exchange was repeated often.

A couple of monkeys

We were all matched up for this family first. Daddy looking like he did every Sunday, handsome in one of his church suits. Mom looking very pretty with a new perm in her hair and her signature hot pink lipstick.

Pretty in Pink by COVERGIRL®. I remember when the color was discontinued, and my mother went from store to store, replenishing her supply. She stored the lipsticks in the refrigerator after she heard that would keep them fresh longer. Vegetables and lipstick. Interestingly, she was adamantly against the wearing of makeup. She thought it made women look cheap. The exception was the lipstick; somehow this was fine.

Then there was big brother, Jonathan, a skinny fourteen-year-old, who would rather have been anywhere else in the world, and ten-year-old me.

The photographer was set up in the church fellowship hall. Smells of coffee and Krispy Kreme doughnuts filled every inch. I loved that smell—the smell of church being over and letting the wiggles out.

I watched each family gathering up its children and taking turns sitting in front of the brown, marbled backdrop for the photo. When it was our turn, I got the special seat on the stool. The photographer's assistant spun it higher and higher to make sure I was the right height and made me laugh a lot to get me ready for the picture.

It was when we got the picture back that I first saw it. What I saw was me, standing out, next to three people who looked so much like each other. My pale skin and blue eyes were a stark contrast to the darker skinned, brown-eyed people with me.

I know what you're thinking. You're thinking that I didn't really look that different from them at all. You don't see the big fuss. I look at it now and feel the same, but somehow and for some reason, I saw it then. I saw someone different. I can't explain how or why, but it hit me like something I had always known, and finally had proof of. The missing link. For me, the image may just as well have been this one:

The Butler family and their lovely Korean baby

I sat there and studied it, and I was even kidding when I pointed it out to my mother and said, "I must be adopted."

Well, you would think I had just asked my mother if she was a virgin when she got married. It did not go over well. I wasn't sure what I had asked that was so horrible, but I got a resounding "No!" and immediately felt very bad that I had said it.

But, the feeling stuck with me, so I had to test it out on my Daddy when he came home from work. I waited for him in the driveway, and when he pulled up from a long day in his dentist office with his patients. He flashed his lights at me as I jumped up and down and waved.

"Hey, Daddy, our pictures came in from the church!"

"Oh, that's so nice. Let me take a look." He rolled up the windows, and I skipped from foot to foot, waiting for him to emerge from his car.

"Yes!" I said, very pointedly handing it over to him, "take a good look and tell me what you notice about it."

He pushed his glasses further up his nose and pretended to examine the picture very seriously.

"Well, I see a very good-looking man. Oh, that's me! "

"Daddy!"

He smiled and returned his focus to the picture, "I see your mother is there and OH, yes, there it is, two monkeys!"

"No, Daddy," I sighed, "look at me. Don't I look different?"

"Different from what?" he asked, removing his glasses and handing the picture back to me. He started to walk into the house.

"Me, I look so different from y'all, look again." I thrust the image at him.

"Elizabeth," he stopped and looked down at me. He was tired from a long day at work and clearly didn't see the need for this interrogation. "You look fine just the way you are."

"Well, I think I look like I'm adopted or something."

"Oh, monkey," he stopped and turned back to look at me, "Why would you say such a ridiculous thing?"

We looked at each other, and he clearly had lost his patience with this conversation. "Don't be silly. Come on now, your mother will be ready for dinner."

He walked into the house and left me holding the picture. And an idea.

I remember this well. I remember thinking something wasn't right. I had done something wrong, and I couldn't figure out why it made my stomach hurt just a little bit. And then I did a very grown up thing. I decided something. I decided they were lying to me.

A seed was planted that day and it grew. It grew without even having to tend it. It took over a little place in my heart, or maybe just in my ears, and whispered to me, "Something is different here."

WHO'S YOUR MOMMA, CHILD?

Pitt Street in The Old Village of Mount Pleasant.
My father's building in the center

I was born in 1968 in Charleston, South Carolina. I was raised across the harbor in Mount Pleasant. Still a modest, lovely, little town when I was born, its one-block downtown known as the Old Village easily supported its population of 7,000 people. Pitt Street was the heart of this charming town and supported everyone's needs.

Beyond the Old Village were farms and tomato fields, the remnants of old pecan plantations and the hint of growth that would take over this once sleepy city by the time I was an adult. It was the beginning of the end of Mount Pleasant's charms that would provide the backdrop of my childhood.

My mother, Katherine Donaldson, was a Mount Pleasant girl, born into a family that could trace its ancestry to several of the first Charlestonians who settled in the area in the 1680s. The names Legare, Lucas, and Simons filled out her family tree, extending our roots deep into the founding of this colony.

Katherine was the third child and second daughter of Robert and Catherine Donaldson. Her birth would claim the life of her mother and leave her father sadly widowed with two toddlers and an infant. Her grandmother, whom everyone called Mamie, stepped in and took my mother to live with her. Mamie sent her teenaged daughter, Rosalee, my mother's aunt, the few short blocks down the street to help her brother-in-law care for the other children. It wasn't long before Rosalee was married to Katherine's father and had two more children to add to the family.

This was a family strategy that Mamie was very familiar with and would have probably encouraged, wanting to keep her family bloodline intact. When Mamie was twelve, her father drowned, leaving her mother with three children to raise alone. As the eldest, Mamie was sent to a Charleston boarding school. Soon after, her mother married her father's brother.

My mother did not return to her father's home full time to live with her brother and sisters and her aunt/stepmother for many years. Perhaps Mamie was worried that Robert would be unable to properly care for her as she grew into a busy toddler and then an active little girl. She continued to live with Mamie and Mamie's bachelor son, Legare. Her life was quiet, and she was raised more as an only child. It suited—*or perhaps created*—her nature as a contentedly solitary person.

She was frequently sent to join the larger family dinners down the street. She did not enjoy having to wait at the table until everyone finished eating. Watching her father and aunt/stepmother enjoying the after-dinner cigarettes. She would have to wait to escape until the cigarette butts were crushed into the dinner plates. She always hated the smell of cigarettes and the images this conjured up for her.

Once my mother entered high school, Mamie decided that it would be better for Katherine to move back in with her father and siblings. Mamie was concerned that her granddaughter had been separated from them too long. Everyone agreed that it would be best to have all of the siblings under one roof—one very crowded roof.

Her father's house was much smaller than Mamie's. Her father, his wife, and now five children were living there, and her father's elderly mother had moved in. There was only one bathroom for eight people.

My mother on the left with her older sister

I imagine my mother was not very comfortable with this sudden shift in arrangements. Her previously quiet house and the sanctity of her own room were now gone, and she was thrust into a busy household with rhythms and routines that were foreign to her. It wasn't long before she was back every weekend at Mamie's house.

My mother excelled in school, winning academic awards that allowed her visits and tours of South Carolina colleges, but her family was unable to afford the luxury of sending its female members off for higher education. After high school, she worked for the Village Shop, the fancy dress clothier on Pitt Street, right in the heart of her town, happily dressing women for parties and social events that she preferred not to attend. The idea of social events unnerved her. She would rather stay home and listen to her records and read her romance novels. She would watch her paychecks go right back into the hands of her employers as the beautiful dresses on the racks tempted her. Her uncle teased her that she needed a job at the Post Office so she could at least bring home something useful from work.

Later she took a job in Charleston at the local paper handling the classified ads. She was content in her job, enjoying weekends on the beaches, casually dating some of the boys she knew, teaching Sunday school at the Presbyterian Church, and singing in the choir.

PAPA'S GOT A BRAND NEW BAG

While my mother was lounging on Charleston beaches or taking boat rides to Crab Bank to hunt for shark's teeth and old Civil War musket balls, my father, John Butler, was growing up on a farm in the mid-state area of South Carolina. When they were not in school, my father and his older sister, Elizabeth, spent their days tending to the animals, running around fields of cotton, and listening to the songs of the field hands who worked the land. It was the Great Depression. Dad's father, Lonnie, got a job with the Works Progress Administration helping construct South Carolina's highways to support the family throughout this challenging time. His mother, Beulah, was an English teacher.

My Dad and aunt grew up in a tiny, white, Victorian farmhouse built by their grandfather. The kitchen was a separate building located behind the main house until my father was in high school. Together, he and his father enclosed an old back porch to accommodate a new, modern kitchen. They did not have indoor plumbing until my father was in his twenties.

Although education was very important to the Butler family, they did not have the money to send my father to a four-year college, so he started his higher education at Spartanburg Junior College. The first spark of my father's entrepreneurial life happened there. He was one of the few students who had a car. He drove into town once a week to buy snacks and sodas from the local grocery store and brought them back to sell to his fellow students.

Soon, World War II broke out, and my father signed up for service in the US Navy. He never saw active duty because of his poor eyesight, so he worked as a medic, stationed in Virginia. He spent his furloughs in New York City, seeing the sights and loving the shows the Rockettes performed at Radio City Music Hall.

The GI Bill sent him to college and medical school, where he studied dentistry. In 1959, my father became the second dentist to set up shop in the quiet city of Mount Pleasant. His practice grew, and his keen sense of business acumen found him purchasing the largest building in the heart of the Old Village, right at the end of Pitt Street. He took this three-story, imposing feature, moved his offices into the first floor, and rented out apartment spaces above. This sparked a love of real estate that was never far from my father's mind.

My father's move into town caught everyone's attention; the new bachelor dentist with a handsome face, quick to smile, and easy to talk to. He quickly made friends with his fellow shop owners on Pitt Street. They all gathered for an early morning cup of coffee at Coleman's Hardware Store before the "Open for Business" signs were hung out.

He was sweet and funny, and I have never heard anything other than a kind word said about my Daddy. A catch for any woman to be sure, but my mother quickly snatched up this eligible bachelor.

I always loved to hear the story of the first time Dad took Mom to meet his family up on the farm. They left right after church in Mount Pleasant and Mom had chosen to wear a new suit with a fur collar and a striking pillbox hat in an identical color. She was the height of fashion with her white gloves and leather clutch bag. When she arrived, her future Mother-in-law greeted her wearing a calico dress and an apron and served Barbeque. Mom would always look back on this memory and laugh at what a spectacle she must have looked like to these people she would grow to love.

Daddy with his parents and sister, Elizabeth 1959

Late to the marriage game, at twenty-seven, my mother was a good match for my father, eleven years her senior, who was ready to start a family. They married in 1963 in a small service in the Mount Pleasant Presbyterian Church, with a reception at her father's home.

My parents bought the most charming house one door down from my father's office. It was a wooden, white, two-story home nestled behind a white picket fence. From its full front porch, you could sit and watch all the activity of Pitt Street and see who was coming and going. Anything my mother needed was, literally, one block away; from groceries to the pharmacy, to clothing, even her church, was down the street.

I can remember walking to church on Sunday mornings, my brother and I following my parents, watching my mother's legs in her modestly high heels clicking down the sidewalk. Once we got to church, we sat in our pew, always the last pew in the church. Mom preferred the very back so that we could get out quickly when it was over. God forbid someone was sitting in OUR pew. Once you sat, you did not move. You looked straight ahead. You were not even allowed to look behind you to see the other parishioners coming in and what they were doing or wearing, even if they laughed or did something else that made you just die to turn around and look. Stare straight ahead.

My parents spent their newlywed weekends up at Dad's family farm, visiting and enjoying time out on Lake Santee in his boat. Daddy was an excellent water skier. He was a patient teacher of the sport and while my mother had no intention of getting her hair wet, his younger cousins were eager to give it a try.

Soon, though, my mother shifted her husband's focus back to the home life she wanted to create. She was not content heading out of town every weekend, spending time at the family farm that his sister, Elizabeth, now called home. She wanted to stay in Mount Pleasant, going to church on Sundays and teaching her Sunday School classes. Of course, my sweet father bent to the wishes of his new wife. He took great pride in becoming an active church member, even acting as the church treasurer for several years.

Their only son, Jonathan, was born in their first year of marriage, one month before their wedding anniversary. It was a difficult birth for my mother. The labor was long, and no one had truly prepared my mother for child birth. Being raised by a grandmother with high Victorian ideals of "things you didn't speak of" left this aspect of womanhood shrouded in mystery.

No doubt, thoughts of her own mother's demise in childbirth added to my mother's fears. She adamantly announced to my father that she would not be having any more children. My father hoped for a larger family, specifically, a little girl. So they adopted me in the summer of 1968, when my older brother was four-and-a-half.

It was a scorching hot August day in South Carolina. Along with my Aunt Elizabeth, my namesake, the four of them made the two-hour drive to pick up their new baby girl in the city of Columbia. The drive was long in the heat of my Daddy's huge, green Ford sedan.

We had that car for a long time. It eventually became my mother's car, and I spent a lot of time riding from errand to errand with her until I went to school. One day, we were in Grant's department store, and I had my eye on a doll. Her name was Bizzie Lizzie, and she came with a feather duster, a tiny ironing board and a vacuum cleaner. (and a very short skirt, just exactly what was the message they were sending little girls?) I begged and begged for that doll, and, finally, Mom agreed to buy it for me.

I mean, really, who designed this doll, Hugh Hefner?

The three of us climbed back into the big green Ford, and I decided that Bizzie Lizzie would sit next to me in the front seat. No one wore seat belts back then, but I got it in my head that she and I would be safer with one on. I pulled the belt around us and was buckling it in next to Bizzie Lizzie. It was rather tight, and once I tried to get settled in, the extra pressure from the seat belt popped the doll's head off. I screamed. Mom was so angry with me. I cried and cried over that doll. She was never quite the same. Her head would just pop right off in the middle of vacuuming.

My aunt and my brother Jonathan stayed outside the Children's Bureau of South Carolina, allowing my mother and father time to meet the agent and their new daughter. It was that situation that allowed my brother to be one of the first to meet me. Aunt Elizabeth spotted a woman walking up with an adorable baby with bright-blue eyes wearing a new, pink, smocked dress. She stopped her and asked if that was the Butler baby. Upon hearing that it was, she stopped to coo over me and let Jonathan meet his new sister.

I was six months old.

Day One in the pink dress someone bought for me

I returned with them that very night to start my life as a Butler. A charmed life lay ahead of me, with privileged parents and every opportunity they could afford to give me.

They named me Elizabeth Legare Butler, crowning me with the names of their ancestors. They toted me about town showing off their newest family member.

My mother's quiet house was quickly filled with well-wishers and the casseroles and cakes that allowed any good Southern woman entrance into a home. My mother kept a carefully handwritten list of all the visitors that came to see the new baby, along with the gifts or food items they had brought, so that gracious thank-you notes could be written. Everybody was so pleased with the new child that Dr. and Mrs. Butler had adopted.

But, I am getting ahead of myself; I won't know any of this for another fifteen years.

**Day two as a Butler, meeting Mamie, my great grandmother.
Jonathan is in every picture taken of me in these first days**

LIKE SANDS THROUGH THE HOURGLASS

My earliest childhood memory takes place around the age of four at the little white house in the Old Village of Mount Pleasant.

From my bedroom window, I watched cars travel slowly up and down Pitt Street as shoppers moved from store to store, greeting each other pleasantly on the streets, stopping to exchange news or gossip. I envied the people heading into the Rexall Drugstore to the lunch counter and wished I could have one of their wonderful grilled cheese sandwiches and a fountain Cherry Coke. I waited patiently to see my father walking home from his office to have lunch with Mom and me as he did every day. When I finally saw him strolling up the block, I ran from my window and flew down the stairs just in time for him to enter so that I could jump into his arms and be carried into the kitchen for our bologna and apple sandwiches, lightly smeared with mayonnaise, a perfect lunch.

By the time I was five, we had moved from the little white house in the bustling, downtown neighborhood to a house my parents built on a quiet private road called Rue De Muckle, on a deep-water lot in old Mount Pleasant. If you didn't know where the street was, you might drive right past it on your way to the public boat landing located right near the entrance.

This entire street was occupied by one family, The Royals. Each sibling owned at least an acre and all but one of them had built a house on it. Noreen and Robert owned the lot in the dead center of all the brothers and they were thinking about selling it. When my Mother heard about this she set her mind to wanting to live there. She knew Noreen Royall quite well. Noreen made my parents' wedding cake. She operated her cake business out of a small house directly behind her home on Hibben Street in the Old Village.

Mom remembered having to pick up the cake the day before her wedding and gently move it from Noreen's house to her father's where the reception would be held. Her friend Bootsie gave her a ride. Bootsie drove a Cadillac and my already nervous mother was even more terrified she would drop this cake in her friend's fancy car. They giggled nervously the entire way, Bootsie slowly navigating every bump and curve of Pitt Street and Mom holding her cake, intoxicated by the smells of butter cream and the dreams of her future life as Mrs. Dr. J.M. Butler.

Wedding Day 1963

I used to love going to the construction site and seeing the beginnings of our new home. Even to this day, the smell of new cut lumber is the most satisfying and comforting aroma. It was the scent of new beginnings. Daddy walked around the skeleton of our soon-to-be home, proudly showing me all the rooms.

I was given the bedroom at the back of the house, overlooking the water. I couldn't wait for it to be finished so that I could sleep there, wake up to the sounds and smells of the creek, and watch the boats and water skiers fly past. Even though I was only five, my mother gave me the opportunity to choose my own room color. I chose a pink that will go down in the family annals as "Pepto Pink" because of its striking resemblance to the medicine. Mom always regretted letting me choose, but in the end, I had a pink room with pink-and-white shag carpeting.

Just down the creek from the house was the heart of Shem Creek's industry, where shrimp boats still dock every afternoon with their wares. Seagulls filled the air above the boats, porpoises surrounded them, and if the wind was blowing just right, you smelled it—salt fish and pluff mud, the perfume of my childhood.

Some of our most exciting moments were spent spotting the beautiful porpoises making their way downstream. Whoever spotted one would shout through the big house to alert the others, and everyone rushed out to catch the graceful creature arching its body out of the water for the briefest glimpse as it gracefully glided down our creek.

My dentist father named the property Tooth Acre.

It seemed like the most perfect life lay ahead of us.

What I didn't realize amidst all of the excitement of the big move was that my childhood had taken a big turn, from town to country. Even though we moved less than one mile away, the four lane bustling Coleman Boulevard cut my path to The Old Village. I was trapped on the wrong side. I was not old enough to cross. I could take my bike to the end of our road and watch the cars and trucks zipping by, stopping me in my tracks. Living on a private road meant no neighborhood children to play with. If I was not lucky enough to be invited to my friends' houses on the weekends,

I was alone. This was torture. I loved to play with my friends and I was often lonely. I was the only child I knew who counted the days until school started so I could be gone. I could hang out with my friends, and my days were surrounded by people.

Who left that Hippity Hop* in the front yard... oh that's me

In the summertime and on weekends, my mother didn't allow me to call my friends too often to avoid being a nuisance to the other mothers, so I patiently waited until the appropriate time in the morning to call. The yellow Trimline phone hanging on the kitchen wall was my chance for escape and rescue. *Please be home, please be home, please answer the phone and say I can come over to play.*

More often than not, my friends were waiting for me to call, and off I went, if I could get mom to give me a ride to their houses. I was always jealous when I called to see what my friends were doing, only to hear their mothers say that they were off in the neighborhood.

Despite the fact that I was surrounded by natural beauty, my young heart dreamt of different things. I wanted to be out in the street playing with friends or playing Kick-the-Can with the neighborhood children until the voices of our parents wafted through the quickly darkening sky, beckoning us home.

I spent my childhood in my room or outside but mainly I spent it in my imagination. I retreated to the large live oak trees surrounding our house. I scaled them to their highest branches and spent my days reading. I descended with a head full of new stories and acted them out in our large backyard.

When we moved in, my father built a floating dock for us. I spent hours out there, dangling my feet over the edge, waiting for a tiny slap of seawater to tickle the bottoms of my feet. I pretended to be on a barge captured by pirates or sailing away, escaping the evil queen as Snow White, rescued by dwarves and loved by a handsome stranger or even as the runaway Huck Finn, exploring the Mississippi.

I played alone outside most of the day, but I was never really alone. I had all kinds of imaginary friends to play with me. We had excellent adventures exploring the acres that surrounded my home. There were five acres total on our street and four houses, including ours. The other houses were lived in by older couples whose children had already moved away and had children of their own. My imaginary friends and I spied on these poor old people and documented their lives.

Miss Weech lived to our right. She had a large sheepdog that was old and content to pad around behind her from room to room. He hated me and spoiled my spying plans by barking if I got to close to her windows. I had to be very careful if I wanted to observe her comings and goings. She watched her Soapbox Opera every day at 2:00. She kept a black-and-white photograph of a lovely girl in her TV room next to her chair. I imagined this was a picture of her long-lost daughter, who had run away to find fame and fortune and never returned to this boredom called Rue De Muckle. Maybe there was the occasional postcard from tropical paradises or huge modern cities. Miss Weech used to make beets for dinner at least once a week. She boiled them, and their aroma was so strong and disgusting that it drove me off as quickly as the dog.

Mrs. Ward and her bachelor son lived to the left. He was a potter. He had a store in Mount Pleasant where he sold his pots and pieces of small art. I watched him throwing pots in a room that once served as a screened porch at the back of their house.

He was a very large man, and I was fascinated that those big hands could make such tiny figurines. Every once in awhile, he would catch me watching and invite me in to see what he was making. I entered shyly and sat talking with him until my mother called for me, wondering why I had disappeared. She would then chastise me for disturbing him while he worked. Every holiday, he had a little gift for me. One Easter, I got two little bunnies, a Mr. and Mrs. Easter Bunny set. Mrs. Bunny had a tiny plastic gem in her ear, like an earring. I always thought it was a real diamond.

Mr. and Mrs. Royall lived on the other side of the Ward's home. They were the hardest to spy on, but that didn't stop me from trying. They had a family room on the second story of their home and stayed up there watching TV unless they were working in their small vegetable garden. They must have had bionic ears because they always heard me coming up to watch them.

Mrs. Royall saved soup labels for me. My school collected them for fund-raising. Every time she caught me sneaking up she would call me up to the kitchen and give me a huge stack of labels. I began to think they only ate soup, especially split pea with ham.

WHAT'S UP, PUSSYCAT?

Like all the other mothers I knew, my mother stayed home to raise her children. She was a good homemaker. Our home was always perfectly clean and tidy. She carefully watched her household budget, planning her shopping to make the most out of every dime. She carefully rationed our food, especially snacks or treats that were extravagant, like gum. If she had gum and you had somehow withered her down to getting a piece, she cut it in half. She even made all my clothes. Dinner was cooked and on the table promptly at 5:30 when Daddy pulled into the driveway from a long day being the town dentist. After dinner, she went to bed with a book and was not to be bothered.

Housekeeping was how my mother showed her love for her family. It didn't come from hugs and kisses or tucking you into bed at night and talking about your feelings. Your feelings were not important. What was important was being obedient, doing well in school, and making a good name for yourself in the community. Those were the pinnacles of success.

I know my mother had great pride in her home and her things. It was, and still is, very important to her. I know that keeping us nicely dressed and presentable was expected of her. She did a wonderful job with all that. But a hug would have been nice or even a touch.

As I became an adult, I came to the conclusion that my mother certainly had a lot of affection and love for me, but I was always left with the notion that these feelings were somewhat of a burden to her. She was unable to express them and too much emotion made her uncomfortable. Oddly enough, when I was much older, I learned the truth of this life lesson from her cat, Blackie.

Blackie was not originally my mother's cat. She belonged to the neighbor. My mother spent her life in her garden, and this cat was a frequent visitor. So, of course, she fed it.

"That cat won't leave me alone," she complained during one of our weekly phone calls, "I was damn near killed tripping over it in the garden today."

"Mom, if you didn't feed it, it wouldn't be there in the first place."

"Of course I have to feed it, Elizabeth! It's so skinny and Prissy, next door, has nothing to do with it. It just lives outside all the time, the poor thing."

"You only have yourself to blame, Mom."

Soon the cat was coming inside.

"Mom!" I exclaimed as the cat flew off a chair when I entered the house for a visit. "The cat got in the house."

"Well, of course he is, Elizabeth, I let him in," she called from the kitchen.

"Mom."

"It was raining, Elizabeth. Blackie can't stay out in all that rain."

"Oh, God, Mom, is this a flea?" I walked into the kitchen scratching my ankle.

"Damnit, now I called Prissy and told her that cat had fleas and you know what she said to me?"

"I can't imagine."

"She said I could have the cat. 'HAVE the cat?' I said, 'I don't want a cat!'"

"Mom," I was looking at the floor in the kitchen. There was a plastic placemat on the floor and three small bowls with different kinds of cat food in them. "How much does this cat eat?"

"Oh, that damn cat is so picky. One day he likes one type of food and the next he turns his nose up at it. I never know which one he'll eat, so I put down all three. I tell you, I'm sick of it."

"You know, Mom, if it gets hungry enough, it will eat anything you put down there."

"Now, I can't do that to the poor cat," she looked at me with disgust.

HAIR TODAY GONE TOMORROW

While I was young girl, busy at play, I wore a baby blanket on my head, held in place with metal clips from my mother's dressing table. It was my "hair." Being born with a head full of thick, light-brown, curly hair might have seemed like an exciting feature to have for a young girl, but to my mother, it was a tangled mass that she could not control.

When I was four, I was taken to the same barber as my brother. As soon as the words, "Look at that rat's nest! You need a haircut," came out of my mother's mouth, I begged and pleaded not to go.

All I wanted was the long hair and pigtails that my friends had or that I saw on television. When Laura Ingalls ran through the field of wildflowers at the beginning of *Little House on The Prairie* with her braids flying or Marcia tossed her long golden hair over her shoulder on The Brady Bunch my heart clenched with envy. I did not want to look like a boy. My imploration was always denied, and the walks to the barber dragged my shoulders closer to the ground, with my head down, trying not to cry. But cry I did, the entire time. As soon as I sat in the hard, plastic booster seat that wobbled on top of the old black leather chair, the barber started pumping up the base to raise me to the dreaded height that would mean the end of any hope of growing my hair out. The scissors came out, and the razor shaved around my ears and up my neck. After I reached the age of four, every single Christmas list began with two words: Long Hair. Surely, Santa had the magic to compel my mother to let it be.

My wish was finally granted at the age of nine when, on Christmas morning, in front of the tree was a pink box with the word *JULIETTE* across the top. Inside on a Styrofoam head painted with rosy cheeks and big blue eyes with long painted lashes sat a dark-brown wig with straight, shoulder-length hair and bangs.

I was transfixed. My long hair had arrived. Santa had heard my prayers and knowing that he could not make hair grow overnight, *(really he can fly all over the world in one night, but grow hair, WHOA little lady…)* granted me the temporary beauty of LONG hair. That wig came out of the box and landed on my head, where it stayed for the rest of the day. What was, at first, very funny to my family became a nuisance as I refused to remove it, even to go to Mamie's house for the expected family Christmas day visit. All the aunts and cousins were there, and I wanted to show them my new luscious locks. Once everyone saw how beautiful my long hair was, I would be able to grow my own hair out, I just knew it, so I smiled and tossed my beautiful hair imagining sunlight dancing on every strand.

The real fight came when I tried to wear the wig to school or tried to sneak it into my book bag. I lost those battles, but the wig went right back on my head the minute I came home every day. I wore it and brushed it until the hair started falling out of the top, leaving the skullcap peeking out. Like a desperate aging male I tried a comb over and tried pinning it in place, but the Juliette continued to shed. *I could have been Benjamin Franklin for Halloween.* That was fine with me; I just wore a hat with it.

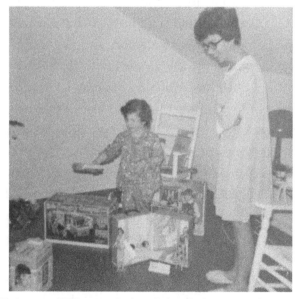

Christmas 1975, my wig box is in the bottom left corner

One day, I came home and the wig was gone. I panicked. Where did it go? Where could I have possibly left it? I ran to my mother in tears. She had no idea, she said. I should take better care of my things. I accused her of hiding it from me, but she adamantly denied this. It was years before I realized that she had thrown it away. I begged for another but was denied. My trips to the barber continued. The older I got the more I heard, "Excuse me young man," or "Why thank you, young man," everywhere we went.

Jonathan, my great grandmother Mamie, and me on Christmas 1977, the Juliette on my head. I looked great!

Me at 15. Is that a mullet waiting to happen? Even the pearls and the slightly puffed sleeves didn't stop people from calling me young man. Interestingly enough I look exactly like my son Aiden in his 15th year. We even had the same haircut...no, his was better.

Aidan at 15, nice hair...

HE AIN'T HEAVY, HE'S MY BROTHER

My insecurities, beginning with my hair and the way I thought I looked, started to take a toll on me.

It didn't help that my brother was the clear winner of my parents' vocal adorations. Jonathan could do no wrong as the extremely bright boy who excelled at everything he tried. His grades always had him at the top of his class. Despite being four years behind him in our tiny private school, I would still enter any first day of class to hear, "Oh, my, are you JONATHAN Butler's SISTER? I expect great things of you." *Awesome!*

I wasn't a bad student, but I wasn't Jonathan. I could never compete, but I was expected to. My father had been the valedictorian and my mother, the salutatorian of their high schools. (Jonathan was valedictorian, too.) So my A's and B's and my "tends to be very talkative" school reviews were not received well at home. Since academia was the standard to which we were judged, I was always lagging behind.

Jonathan was always going to be successful. Everything he did was done with full commitment and attention. When he was a boy and wanted to be a magician, he studied every magic book and saved his money to buy the most elaborate tricks he could afford. When he switched and decided to take up photography as a teen, he studied everything about cameras and developing film. In college, he developed an interest in sports rifle and pistol shooting and learned everything he could about guns. He even made his own bullets and won championships around South Carolina.

Jonathan was twelve-years-old when he took an interest in the stock market. Where other boys had rooms covered in posters with fast cars or barely clad swimsuit models, he had a white board with stock trends. He gave my father money to invest for him since he was too young to solicit his own stockbroker..

He was the first kid in our school to own a personal computer, and he taught the teachers how to use it. *Yes, you read that correctly, my 13 year old brother was teaching his teachers. I wonder how many of them were thinking "this thing will never take off…"*

Oh, you're Jonathan Butler's sister?

When I was in the third grade, I decided that I liked writing capital "L's" better than capital "E's," so I announced to my family and friends that everyone should now call me Liz. Jonathan was the only one in the family who indulged me.

"Liz, come look at the computer, watch this." He wrote a simple program, and the screen flashed symbols on and off and all around.

"That's cool!" I said, holding my Barbie and admiring her long, straight, blonde hair.

"Sit down, I'll show you how to do it," he offered excitedly.

"Nah, I've tied my Barbie sports car to the back of my bicycle, and I'm going to ride up and down the street so she can feel the wind in her beautiful long hair."

"Oh, come on, Liz, the computer is so much cooler. Look here, for every page in this manual that you learn, I'll give you a nickel."

I looked at the computer, it's green screen flashing at me from the corner desk in my brother's room that smelled like socks. I wrinkled my nose in disgust and clicked my tongue on the roof of my mouth, "Nah, I don't want to," and off I skipped.

Now, I think… Stupid bitch. That would have really come in handy in later life.

My brother will be a millionaire many times over and retired by the time he is 40 thanks to the Stock Exchange and a computer.

CAN I GET A WITNESS?

I moved along in my young life constantly watching and listening and started to notice all the ways I was different. I carefully documented these differences in my many *Precious Moment's* diaries. I would fill them with overly dramatic interpretations of my life and times. I often thought of running away. That would solve everything. I could hide out in my girlfriends' homes, living in closets and surviving on scrap food they brought me from their dinner tables. Exactly what I would do after that was never really clear, but it didn't matter, it was the thrill of the escape that peaked my interest. Of course the next exciting moment would be the thrill of reunion where tears were shed and I was begged to return to the household promised all the love and attention I needed. *Maybe I could get a new wardrobe while I was at it.*

There were moments when I thought that there would be a certain phase of my life during which my mother and I would bond *(I still have these moments)*. I would finally have the key to unlock her heart. This would be the moment that would make us friends. Our little secret. We would share secret glances my brother could never understand. The closer I got to twelve, the more I thought this would happen.

This was the transformative year when I would become a *woman*, according to all the hype. My girlfriends were all coming to me with the embarrassing moment they had with their mothers and the long talks that followed about their bodies. I "ewwed" and rolled my eyes with all of them, but secretly I hoped for this moment. I could handle the embarrassment. This would break the ice.

I'll never forget the day I came home from school to find a pamphlet on my bed. There was the drawing of a girl on a bicycle, her ponytail flying out behind her as she metaphorically "cycled" into her future. She seemed very happy about it *(and her hair was fabulous)*. Under the pamphlet was a box of maxi pads and a strange-looking elastic belt. This was my introduction to womanhood. This was my moment, lost.

Every Monday afternoon from the time I was nine until I was thirteen, I was in Mrs. Schraibman's house for piano lessons promptly at 3 p.m. Her piano was in the front room of the house, and I remember being in a bright sunny room with a large bay window at my back. Oh, how the light and shadows that danced across the piano from that window tempted me to look around and see what was going on outside.

Mrs. Schraibman grew to love me and I her, very much. She was thrilled with my natural piano abilities, and she delighted in hearing the far-flung stories about what I had "done" throughout the week since our last lesson. She called me her star, and I believed her.

Upon discovering that I liked to sing, she had a present for me the following Monday—a songbook from the musical *Annie*. She wanted to hear me sing "Tomorrow." I was terribly shy, and I wouldn't do it until she left the room so that I wouldn't feel her staring at me. Now, I couldn't just sing, I could SING. I surprised myself as much as Mrs. Schraibman, and she insisted that I perform this at our next recital. I didn't tell a soul, for two reasons: (1) I could still chicken out and (2) I didn't want anyone at home to second-guess this decision and make me worry that I would embarrass anyone if I couldn't carry a tune.

The day of the recital came. We met in a small hall at the local music store in downtown Charleston. I don't remember a thing about what that room looked like; I was so in-my-head crazy nervous. I was next to last to perform, so I had even longer to worry about it. The worst part was when my classmate, Dick Rieger, walked into the room. His younger sister was also a student of Mrs. Schraibman's. This was a disaster. If I messed up, I would not just be the laughing stock of the other pianists, news of the fiasco would inevitably get back to my SCHOOL.

I walked up to the piano and played my first piece, the one chosen to show off my newest abilities. Then came "Tomorrow." Introduction. SING. I remember glancing quickly at Dick Rieger before I opened my mouth. He was wearing a brown sport coat and was looking down at his program, the pain of boredom all over his face. With the first note that I belted out, his head whipped up, along with those of so many other previously resigned parents and siblings. At the end of my solo, everyone in the room burst into surprised applause, and I was intoxicated with the attention. I was doing something that was special and I knew it. Now, I had something Jonathan didn't have. I didn't have to be just like him; I could just be me. This was such a feeling of relief for me. My burden of second best was lifted.

Soon after that I was asked by a member of our church to recite a monologue at the Christmas pageant to be held in the Fellowship Hall one Sunday evening before the holidays. Mrs. Huger was my Sunday School teacher, and she saw first-hand my flare for the dramatic *(my star quality?)*. I eagerly accepted.

She invited me to her house one afternoon for rehearsals. Mrs. Huger's family owned all the Krispy Kreme doughnut shops in town. Her house was big and beautiful, with many windows that looked out over a vast acreage. And it smelled like a doughnut. That was heaven right there.

Mrs. Huger was very excited about the show. I was good at memorizing things. My years at the piano had prepared me for that.

"Elizabeth, you are doing a wonderful job. Why, you are just a natural born actress!" she declared, delighted with my run-through and interpretation of the little piece.

"Thank you." I could feel myself blushing, my ears on fire.

"I'll be able to say 'I knew her well' once you are famous."

After Mrs. Huger's death, the family sold the house and all the property to the local hospital. The house still stands, but the beauty around it is all but gone. The towering hospital building shadows that lovely home. Today this property sits across the street from my children's elementary school, and I think of sweet and gracious Mrs. Huger often. But in the South your family is defined by its drama; this is why it's tucked away so deeply in a family's emotional vault. Not only is it never spoken of, it can be entirely denied with believability. Yet someone always remembers; they sigh deeply and look at something just past you, and let the drama unfold. I heard that one of Mrs. Huger's sons had developed a psychosis that had him returning home to have her care for him. One morning he had a relapse and pulled a knife on his mother. She ended up running across the street to the school in her nightgown screaming for help.

I looked forward to my performance that night, to show my family that I was ready to be a star. How could school be the most important thing if I had all this talent just waiting to be discovered? Surely, this would be an eye opener for them too! *THIS is what we can do with Elizabeth, they will think.* I remember doing that little monologue at the church and seeing my father sitting on the aisle. Because he was leaning over so far to make sure he saw everything that I did, I was afraid he would fall out of the chair.

I'd found my calling, something I loved and I was good at it. I no longer had to compete with my brother. *Whew, cause that was not working out so well.* I would never be as smart as he was or as studious, but that no longer mattered. I would be the family actress and singer! Now what?

It was a frustrating time for me, having all these creative ideas and not knowing how to harness them. I begged to be sent to acting classes, but my family considered that a waste of money. It was most important not to make a spectacle of oneself. My job as Elizabeth Butler was to go to school, be a straight "A" student, and go to college, where I would meet my husband, get married, and raise children who would be straight "A" students, continuing the cycle. My opportunity to be just as important to my parents as Jonathan was slipping away. Why couldn't I make them understand?

As I traveled through my childhood, drama never left me. I embraced it. When my mother tuned into *Days of Our Lives*, I would sneak into the room to watch, peeking behind the brown plaid recliner, spying on the lives of the residents of Salem. Daddy let me stay up late to watch *Dallas* on Friday nights. I was fascinated with the stories of these people. I knew no one like them. These characters and their adventures painted even richer colors on the backdrop of my imaginative play. When they were falling in love, so was I. When they were in danger, I would act that out, too. I would arrive at the dinner table late *(dramatic entrance, please)* wearing every piece of play jewelry I owned and some sort of gown *(don't we dress for dinner? Are we farmers?)* I would be greeted with stares and laughter and the occasional, "where did you get the lipstick?" *Well, it makes my blue eyes bluer don't you think???* "Take it off."

For years, when people would ask me what I wanted to be when I grew up I said Marlena Evans. Her character was the beautiful doctor on my mother's soap opera. Most of my family thought that meant I wanted to be a doctor. No, I just wanted to play one on TV.

Then, there was Tammy Amerson.

Tammy Amerson was the local "It" child. She was just one year younger than I was, but she appeared on all the telethons on TV. She was on the local news as minor successes began to come her way—smaller parts on TV and in small-budget movies. Every time she came on the TV, my mom would just gush.

"Oh, there is that Tammy Amerson," Mom would say, stopping whatever she was doing to watch her, to look at HER.

"I could do that, "I suggested. "How do you get to be on those shows? I can sing and play the piano, too."

"Oh, Elizabeth, you're no Tammy Amerson."

I hated Tammy Amerson, not just because she was talented, although she was. I hated her because my mother loved her. My mother was impressed with her talents and just knew she would be a star.

"Just keep an eye on that one," she would say "She'll be someone one day."

Well, what about me? Why couldn't my mother see what Tammy's mother saw? I was here and ready to go.

Look at me and see that I am different and tell me that it's OK.

SPIRIT

I had an aunt on my mother's side, Betty, or Liz, as she asked to be called later. *I totally got that, just like me*, but old habits are hard to break, and I still called her Aunt Betty. She was my favorite. She was a bit of scandal in the family, having divorced my great-uncle, not to mention that my great-uncle was not her first husband.

Where ARE the smelling salts?

She was beautiful (explains the trail of broken hearts left behind her); she was sweet; and she adored me. She kept up with everything I did. When I was acting in local theatre, she clipped every review of mine from the paper and saved it for me. She once wrote a letter to the editor of our newspaper, praising the show I was in and my performance. She never missed an opportunity to support me and love me. I often wonder if she saw a kindred spirit in me, as we were both very different from this family we had been brought into. Our flamboyance and adventurous spirits setting us apart.

She came to see one of my first theatrical leading roles. I was nineteen and playing Annie Sullivan in the *The Miracle Worker*. After the show, I came out of the back stage door. Aunt Betty was standing there, waiting for me. I saw her first with her perfectly coiffed light brown hair and her meticulously applied makeup that made her lively eyes sparkle and shine. She had tears in those eyes when she wrapped me in the warmest embrace, going on and on about how proud she was of me.

She attended the show with her dear friend, Dr. James Ward, a deliciously flamboyant, deeply Southern man, who spoke softly with his lyrical accent but gestured wildly with his hands to emphasize any point he was making. He was one of our family doctors from the Old Village, and I had seen him as a child. He, too, filled my fragile ego with praise and sweet words.

"Elizabeth," he said, "I am so proud of you for breaking out of your shell and doing this. Your parents tried so hard to make you shy." He leaned closer and whispered in my ear, "I knew it wouldn't work."

Many years later, when I lost my Dad, my Aunt Betty called to make sure I was OK.

"You know I love you, sweet girl. I'm coming over to bring you a dinner. I know everyone is bringing food to your mother's house, but I want you to have something, too."

"Thank you, Aunt Betty." I was grateful to hear from her in my sadness. "I do feel so lost without him. I don't know how I'm going to get over it. I'm so glad you called."

"Your Daddy loved you so much, Elizabeth, and he was always so proud of you."

I started to cry.

"Look here, you know your Mother is too, she can't help it if she doesn't know how to say it, but we all know she loves you deeply. I'm proud of you, too, you know. Now that your Daddy is gone, I'm going to be your number one fan." I loved the sound of her voice, deep and gravelly with years of cigarette smoke waiting dangerously in her lungs.

"Yes ma'am, I accept," I laughed.

"You know what I love about you the most?"

"Oh, lord," I really laughed now.

"You've been through a lot. You've had some disappointments, and you made your fair share of mistakes, but no matter what, you always bounced back. You are a strong Southern woman born and raised in Dixie. You bloom wherever you are planted. "

No one in my family had ever, to that day, put a positive spin on my failures. Her words still rise up in my mind whenever I doubt myself, or whenever I feel lost or EVER think of giving up.

In 2016, I turned forty-eight-years old, or, as I prefer, twelve in leap years. I had an app on my iPhone that offered daily inspirational quotes. Much to my delight, this note popped up on my birthday, a special message from my Aunt Betty.

Thanks, Aunt Betty.

DOCKET NUMBER 022968: NATURE V. NURTURE

Family portrait 1980

I was twelve.

It was time for another family portrait. I spent every night in the time between its announcement and the actual date combing my hair every night: 100 strokes. I hoped and prayed that it would grow even just a little so that I could wear a pretty barrette or a comb in my hair and look like the other girls. I was prepared for this picture and had spent all afternoon trying to sneak makeup on my face.

I secretly slipped some lip gloss into my bag, *COVERGIRL® Barely Nude*. Earlier in the week, I had hopped on my bicycle and ridden to the Eckerd drugstore by my house to buy it, but the check-out lady, Mrs. Denney, knew my parents and wouldn't sell it to me, knowing they would disapprove of makeup at my young age.

Seriously! This woman had a granddaughter who did beauty pageants and had been wearing lipstick and rouge since she was 18 months old. She couldn't sell me lip gloss?? It was NUDE for heaven's sake, not cherry red. I could have smeared Vaseline on my lips and gotten the same shine, I just wanted something grown up that sparkled in the light and didn't smell like a scraped elbow or an old bandage. Real lip gloss had the smell of adulthood and freedom. It sat on your lips right below your nose and filled your mind with womanly wiles. Didn't it?

I had to sneak off and pedal, in the last warm days of summer, to the other side of town to find a drugstore where I could buy it without being scolded. *Maybe just two miles but dear god, I bet Tammy Amerson never had to do this! The heat and my perspiration frizzing the ends of the two inches of hair surrounding my head. That had to be a sight for the poor check out girl who probably thought… oh dear, she's going to need a lot more than lip gloss.*

My mother hated this picture. The photographer said something funny. You could see my brother smirking. *I, of course, would never break character.* Mom is laughing with her teeth showing. She hated having her teeth show in pictures. She had braces as a child, but after they removed them, her teeth went back to their original disarray, and she always smiled differently for pictures because of this.

Despite all the imperfections in this latest forced family portrait, what I saw, again, was me. I would place my hand on the photograph and cover my image to see the real family. *How clearly they belonged to one another.* Lifting my hand again to see… the Butler's and their British foreign exchange student, Cordelia McDifferent. It reminded me of how I had felt two years ago, and the old whispers were back in my head.

Look closely, don't you see it? This explains everything. This explains why they don't understand the dreams you have. You are different from them. Look close, look closer.

The photo was shared with family, who went on and on about my brother. The only biological child of the family, he strongly possessed his parents' genes. Everyone in the family loved to comment on his resemblance to my Dad.

I will never forget the debate at Mamie's house over this picture. The aunts were gathered about, filling the air with scents of rose water and body powder, debating whom he took after more, his mother or father. *How grown up. How handsome.*

Eventually my great aunt, Mary Louise, leaned towards me and said, "Well, who do you look like, Elizabeth?" I looked right at her and said, "No one, I guess." It was not heard by anyone but her, so there was no great moment of general unease, but she looked confused for just the slightest moment and stumbled in her reply, "Well, you look like you, and isn't that lovely?" And whatever had planted itself in my heart all those years ago got a little bigger.

I started sharing these feelings with my friends, and they either got on board with this new mystery because, hey it's drama and every teen girl likes that, or they called me crazy.

Every time I thought about it, it grew into a bigger idea. And I would ask again. *Are you sure?*

I chose random times to broach this tender subject.

I also learned very quickly never ever to ask my mother again. Anytime I made a comment, I was cut off quickly and abruptly.

Mom had a short fuse and a quick temper, and the rambunctious, opinionated child that I was tested this on too many occasions.

"Oh, Elizabeth!" *The exasperation in her voice, I hear it as if it were yesterday.* "I just wish you would settle down. I don't understand why you insist on this behavior."

"Well, then, see, I guess I must be adopted," I would reply in my irritation with her.

Electricity would crackle behind her eyes which locked onto me frozen in aggravation, "YOU ARE NOT ADOPTED! I HAVE NEVER HEARD ANYTHING SO RIDICULOUS!"

I shrunk into myself. She didn't think it was funny anymore.

So Daddy was my target if the whispers got to be too loud.

We had a summertime habit of going on bike rides together after dinner while Mom was stuck cleaning the kitchen. We had a particularly good ride one night, and Daddy decided we could go a little further, riding through the Old Village. Those were my favorite rides because it was an adventure, and we could actually run into people we knew. We would wave and say, "HEY," and occasionally, I would see a friend and get to chat for a minute. It was heaven. This is what it was like to live around people.

Our rides led to moments of easy quiet, and the lack of eye contact made more difficult subjects easier to broach.

"Hey, Daddy."

"Hey, what."

"I was thinking about something the other day."

We pedaled along. He wasn't taking any bait, so I had to follow through. "I was just thinking that sometimes I feel so different from Jonathan, I was wondering if I was maybe adopted."

"Elizabeth," he sighed, "why are you always asking questions like this? Why can't we just have a nice quiet bike ride?"

That wasn't a "No."

Pedal on.

Still my thoughts continued to nag me as I got older. I was convinced my parents were keeping something from me, but why? Maybe there was some dark mystery surrounding this alleged adoption that they were sworn to uphold.

Surely I could crack this case. If my favorite literary character, the strawberry blonde Nancy Drew, could do it, so could I. I could investigate. I could talk to people. All I needed were my friends and a blue convertible, just like Nancy.

So, that's what I did, minus the convertible and the good hair. First, I sought out documentation.

Daddy was sitting in his recliner in the den after dinner, reading the evening paper. I sat on the couch next to him.

"Hey, Daddy."

"Hey, what?" he asked from behind the paper

"I know how you could get me to stop asking if I'm adopted."

The paper came down,"This again?"

"Well, how about you show me my birth certificate?"

The paper went back up.

"Daddy...."

"Well, I would but I don't have it; it's at the office."

"You could go get it."

Paper folded back down, "Elizabeth, I was trying to read the paper. I'm not going back out today."

"You could bring it home, tomorrow, though, right?"

Paper back up. Conversation over.

Dad proudly procured the secret document the next day, and much to my disappointment, it was not what I expected at all. There it was, official and even dutifully notarized: my own parents names as Mother and Father. I felt myself deflate. *How could this be? This isn't right.* He looked at me and smiled and said, "There now. We can agree to close this subject for good, can't we?"

This wasn't right. How could I be so wrong? Where were all these feelings coming from? I ran my fingers over the raised seal and, holding back tears of frustration, I gave the document back to him.

OK, so let's have a little aside moment right now. Seriously? Your daughter has been questioning her parentage for YEARS. She is now to the point of asking for proof, and you don't stop, as a parent, and think, "Gee, honey, she sure is asking a lot of questions. Maybe we need to talk to her about this or call a doctor and see what the doctor thinks." Really? THAT wasn't happening? They really thought this would just disappear?

I was fifteen-years-old and full of all the teenage rebellion that makes every young girl such a joy to live with, but I was fueled with a deeper teenage angst. It wasn't enough that "they" just didn't understand me, or still thought of me as a baby, or wouldn't let me have any freedom. I was clearly different from them. That was all there was to it. It was not a generation gap; it was a biological gap *that could immediately be fixed if only I was in the right place.*

The old whispers were back in my head. *"That birth certificate was a forgery,"* they murmured in breathy voices. *"They are lying to you. You have to find the truth. You deserve to know who you are. Everything will be all right once you know the secret. You are not crazy."*

YOU SAY IT BEST WHEN YOU SAY NOTHING AT ALL

Whenever I was alone in the house, I snooped through drawers and looked into private places in my parents' room, hoping to find the smoking gun. The adoption papers *(that would be great)* or the name of the secret doctor who has "those patients" that need to quietly give away their children to loving families in desperate need. A photograph. Yes, that would be a miracle.

I spent hours on the phone working out these theories with my best friend, Lydia. She was hot on the trail with me, the George Fayne to my Nancy Drew. She was the one who lit the fire and stoked it until it was too hot to let alone any longer.

I was sitting in the hallway by my bedroom, painting my toenails a bright red and talking to Lydia on my green Trimline phone. My face was already burning from being on the phone so long with her, and the light-up keypad was scorching my face. I switched ears.

"Mom will never let me come over. She says I've been spending too much time away and I need to stay home."

"Are you kidding me?" She replied. "I'm so bored. What does she want you to be doing?"

"I don't know, nothing. She's just so frustrating. She doesn't like to do anything, so I can't either."

"Another reason why you are adopted."

"Yes! " I laughed. "If we could only prove it. They never go anywhere often enough for me to get a good look around."

"What did you find last time, anything good?" she asked, chomping on something crunchy.

"Nothing. Absolutely nothing. I think everything is at Daddy's office."

"Do you have a key?"

"I am not breaking into the office, Lydia, there is no way."

Then finally, she had a brilliant plan.

"Why don't you just ask them?" Lydia said.

"Where have you been?" I would have rolled my eyes, but I was carefully painting my pinkie toe and it's so small. "I tried that many times over many years. Aren't you listening?"

"I know. So this time, you have to do it differently."

"How, stand on my head? It's not working like that."

"Liz, you need to make them think you already know the truth. You tell them that you have heard this from somebody's parents."

That seemed too easy.

That could not possibly work.

Could it?

I decided to try this out on Daddy the same night. I felt like I could talk to him. It wasn't something we did very often, so there wasn't a lot of background for exactly how to do this.

What if I was right after all? This could get emotional. We didn't do emotion in my family.

At this time of my life, my father had said he loved me once (my mother, never). It was after a particularly moving episode of *Little House on the Prairie*. A daughter had gotten lost from her father, and the reunion scene was very moving. I got up to go to bed when the show was over and was almost out the door when he said it. His voice cracked with emotion. I was so frozen in my tracks that I didn't even turn around. I said it back and ran up to my room. I never forgot that.

Many years later I was alone in my bedroom, getting dressed for my father's funeral. I wondered if I should bother with putting on eye makeup. After all, I'd just cry it off, and there was no need to look worse than I already did.

In this moment of sheer grief, I felt I could not bear the quiet around me. I grabbed the remote control and turned on the television, hoping the noise would soothe me.

The television, at that moment, was playing that very episode of *Little*

House on the Prairie.

Dad was alone in his garden, his happy place, tending the vegetables he grew every year with such pride.

I walked out there and said, "Hey, Daddy, I have to ask you a question."

He paused in his work, leaned on his hoe, and looked at me. "Sure, what is it?"

Do it, Liz, just say it....

"Was I adopted?" My hands were shaking, so I put them in the pockets of my shorts. My heart was beating in my ears, not because I thought he would just spontaneously answer this question, it was the follow-up that was bubbling inside me.

"Now, why are you asking me this?" He said. *(That was a new response.)*

"Well, Mrs. _____ *(of course, I used Lydia's mom)* seems to think so."

I regretted this the moment I said it. Not because I wasn't dying to know if, this time, my ploy would actually work but because I saw the instant wound on my father's sweet face. As if I had shoved him just a little on his chest, the slightest of movements followed by a deflation in his posture. A long, tired sigh escaped from him.

"Well, yes, you are."

BOOM.

I got what I wanted. There it was. I couldn't believe it. All the years of asking and being told "no." Being LIED to. They lied to me. This was my big moment. My victory. My time to scream, I KNEW IT! Fall to my knees in the garden dirt like Scarlett O'Hara, ripping a carrot out of the garden and shaking it violently at the sky, "I will never be ignorant AGAIN!"

Then I saw the tears in my Daddy's eyes. He was as hurt as I was. Well, I don't know what I was feeling. Was it hurt? Was it disappointment?

Whatever it was, I was cut off at the knees. I couldn't rejoice. I had to quickly put that aside and fix what I had just done. This was not what I anticipated. I had heard "NO, NO, NO" for so long. I never thought it would feel this way. I had nowhere to put everything I was feeling. I had never seen my dad cry.

So I said, "Well, then, I'm sure glad they gave me to you." And I hugged him. And we cried a little, but that was weird. We didn't cry in my family, and hugging was nonexistent, so it was awkward. I patted him on the back a bit to break up the moment, and I turned and walked away.

It was a long walk, a half an acre to get back to the house. I kept my head down and watched my bright-red toenails stepping through blades of grass that felt like a thousand tiny snake tongues licking my bare feet, and I never looked back. Not once.

My father and I didn't speak of this moment again for over a year.

OH, WHAT TANGLED WEBS WE WEAVE

I spent the next year talking about it a lot, just not with my parents.

I spent a lot of time thinking about it, but I had nowhere to go. There was nothing in the phone book under *"you just had the rug pulled out from under you, now what?"* No pamphlet for me this time. There was no twelve-step program. I was really all alone with these feelings, and I didn't know what to do.

I felt betrayed, but then I felt guilty for feeling that way. I was angry and then I was so sad. I tried to talk to my friends, but it was hard for them to feel what I was feeling. It's hard at any age to understand that you are not the person you thought you were because of course you are! I was still Elizabeth Butler. I still had the same parents and aunts and uncles. This was still my family… but I didn't have their eyes or their straight hair, and I didn't have their quirks and instincts. I knew that. I always knew that.

They lied to me.

They did worse things than lie to me. They lied and then made me believe that I was the crazy one. *Just look, Elizabeth, here is your birth certificate. Now you can stop this nonsense* LIE, LIE, LIE.

So now whatever seed had been planted when I was at the vulnerable age of ten had a new flower, and it wasn't pretty, it was rotting. Who was the missing link? Would she look just like me? Would she have my dark hair and blues eyes? Would she understand my feelings? That was the new focus. I had to find out more about her. Why did she give me up? What was happening in her life? Was she looking for me? My god, she might have been looking for me! How would I know? There was no one to talk to about this. No one to help me.

This was the elephant in the room that no one spoke of. I often wondered if it made my mother withdraw from me even more than she did before. Now maybe I was dangerous. When would I confront her about this? I have no idea how she felt about it. She never came to me.

Thus began a horrible year.

Many years later, I had the chance to talk with Lydia in between juggling lives, careers, and children. We caught up a little and made the obligatory plans to get together next time we were in the same town. She ended the phone call by revealing to me that for years after I found out I was adopted, she carried great guilt with her. She felt that she had pushed me into confronting my parents and had no idea that the truth would spin me out of control into a full-blown identity crisis. I was surprised to hear this, and I tried to absolve her of any guilt. I was already in the midst of an identity crisis, I told her. The spiral was inevitable.

CRY FOR HELP

I was fifteen.

I just had my world turned upside down. Everything I knew about myself changed. I wasn't who I was told I was. I was from someplace else. I was different. I knew it.

I wanted answers and I couldn't get them. I was scared of what they might reveal. I kept the painful feelings buried. My grades began slipping and my friendships shifting. I was unsure of myself. This was a pressure I did not know how to handle.

I was fifteen.

I was a freshman in high school, still at the same elite little private school I had always attended. I was desperate to get away from the same twenty or so students I had known and been in class with since I was in kindergarten. I wanted a fresh start somewhere else. I wanted to be around people who didn't know me, who did not know that this girl was a joke or that she had been lied to about who she was. I was tired of feeling that everyone had conspired against me to keep this secret, that everyone had betrayed me. I wanted to shed the skin of that pathetic girl and let a new one grow— to reinvent myself without secrets.

I was beginning to lose myself.

I pleaded with my family to allow me to leave my school and go to the large public high school in town. The public school had a theatre department and a choral department. I could actually take classes and study the things I loved. I could have a place to release the screams that threatened to leak out of my mouth, as I was losing the ability to hold them in.

It took me a full year, a tour of the other school, and a meeting with the principal to convince my parents to let me do this. I entered Wando

High School as a sophomore, so excited for my fresh start. I thought that was all I needed. I was doing the only thing I knew to do, the action I was raised to do, pack up all these ugly feelings and pretend they do not exist.

I was sixteen.

It was summer. I was home more and things were tense. I was not in a good place with my mother, who didn't know what to do with her damaged teenaged daughter. I had no escapes. So many friends were away at camp or with their families on vacation, and I just felt alone and sad.

I tried to be gone all the time, to escape, but I couldn't get far enough away. I went for long drives, which didn't help. I felt like a lion in a cage, trapped behind bars and dreaming of the great savannah. I was restless.

I sat alone in my room, reading the stories of other teenaged girls' anxieties in my teen fashion magazines. I found myself particularly drawn to the stories of girls who tried to hurt themselves.

How could anyone do that?

I know exactly why they do it. I know what that darkness feels like when it creeps up behind you, dragging its shadowy fingers up your back and onto your head, squeezing tightly, the weight of it crushing you. It talks to you in a sweet language. "You are hurting, but I can help you make it stop anytime. Drive faster! One quick turn of the wheel and you are in that tree. It's done. And won't they just be sorry that they didn't listen to you. They will cry and tear at their clothing and beg for another chance… or will they? Will they just be relieved? Won't you?"

All of these emotions sat deep inside me. I could feel them trying to get out, pressing against my skull as if a balloon were being blown up inside my brain.

I fought with my parents. The arguments came fast and easy these days. We were at an impasse, me craving more freedom, them trying everything to contain me. We had a stupid argument, the details of which are not important, but the result was that I got grounded. In one heated moment, I had lost my only escape.

One of the reasons I was in trouble was because my parents did not like the crowd I was hanging with. This caused our biggest fight of that summer, as I tried to explain that they were really great kids. As an adult, I have often taken great pleasure in bringing up the names of these "kids" and mentioning their accomplishments. Nurse, Respected Artist, one is even a long-standing member of the South Carolina State House of Representatives.

I spent hours in my room angry. Sad and angry. Hurt and angry.

I wanted desperately to stop those feelings.

The bottle of pills that I took did not stop them.

It made things worse.

It was a horrible scene.

I started to get sick. This was not just falling asleep and never waking up. This was ugly and painful, and I got scared. I called my friend, Molly, to come help me, save me. I wasn't sure what I thought would happen. I was hoping she could sneak me out of the house and I could go somewhere and get better. Walk around and drink lots of coffee like they do in the movies. No one will ever have to know how stupid I was.

Her red Toyota screeched into my driveway; *so much for sneaking.* There was lots of screeching in the driveway that day. *That's my fault,* was all I could think.

I could hear the urgency of the back doorbell ringing. I could hear the heightened voice of Molly, but not just her, I heard other friends too, my god, what had I done.

My parents broke down my door to find me in the room, and Dad screamed at my brother to run to his pharmacy and get something for me. More screeching. *Wow, Jonathan loves me; he's really running out of here!* I remember thinking.

Dad dragged me into my bathroom, *"What did you take! What did you take! What have you done?"* his voice so high pitched, so panicked. He stuck his fingers down my throat trying to make me vomit.

Mom screamed at my friends to get out. More screeching. Too much screaming.

Jonathan returned and I drank something that made me throw up the rest of the day. I remember lying on the cold tile of the bathroom floor, weak from vomiting, the room spinning. It took all the strength I had to sit up and expel the contents of my stomach into the toilet and not all over myself. No doctor was called. This was taken care of in private.

I remember my ears ringing. I was back in my bed, and my father came in to check on me, but I couldn't hear him. He said something and then he turned his back to me and leaned on my door frame wracked with sobs that I could see but couldn't hear. At that moment, I was grateful that I couldn't hear.

I stayed in bed for two days. My father came in frequently to make sure I was still breathing. My mother came in infrequently. I didn't see my brother at all. I've never spoken of this day with him. Ever.

LIGHTHOUSE

I have always thought of my brother as a human lighthouse. Stalwart on an island, towering above us all, his beam of light sweeping over the world around him. If you were lucky enough to have that beam of light land on you, it was warm and inviting, like rays of sunshine. You had his undivided attention, and it was amazing. If that beam passed over you, you might as well be invisible.

Jonathan became an increasingly private person as he got older, so I learned to embrace those moments in the light for as long as I could. He had his friends; he had his hobbies; and he did not seem to need us for emotional support. He was quick-tempered like his mother and easily aggravated. If you pushed too hard for his attention, he snapped. I learned to wait for the light to sweep back around and was smart enough to enjoy it. I learned his facial cues. If you tried to talk to him and he just nodded while you spoke...stop talking, he's not there with you, but if you spoke and his eyebrows rose quickly up into his hairline, keep going, you've got him, hold on, he's with you. I don't think Mom ever figured that out, and there was a year filled with lots of yelling and door slamming and one very memorable, "You can go to hell!"

I was nine. I was sitting in the corner on the landing of our staircase with my coloring books. I liked to sit and color there because I could feel the pulse of the entire house around me. The kitchen was behind me, and the front door was directly in front of me. The upstairs was fully visible through the spindles of the railing that exposed the second-story hallway. I could hear or see everything that might be going on.

I was there, surrounded by coloring books and boxes of crayons, perfecting a drawing, when I heard the worst fight break out between Jonathan and Mom in the kitchen. I pressed my ear to the wall behind me to hear them better and see what all the fussing was about. The loud vibrations tickled my ear.

Yelling was a unique sound in our house. It scared me and rattled the little world I was living in. Jonathan came storming up the stairs past me, scattering my crayons, creating chaos in my coloring world. I had to pull my legs away to avoid being trampled by Mom, hot on his trail, trying to swat at him with a yellow kitchen rag.

Yell. Slam. Yell.

She demanded that he come out of the room.

Silence. The loudest silence I had yet to encounter. I froze.

I was in awe of this amazing show of emotion. I didn't know how I was supposed to react to raised voices in my house.

Mom turned to me. My eyes were wide with wonder at this spectacle.

I thought she was waiting for me to say something. I didn't know what to say, so I blurted out the first thing that popped into my head.

"When will I be old enough to talk to you that way?" I innocently asked, having no idea of the mistake I had just made.

She marched down the stairs to the landing, the yellow kitchen towel wrapped up between her hands, and then bent down so that her nose was almost level with mine. She smelled like the chicken dinner she was making and the pink lipstick that was ever present on her mouth. "NEVER!" she yelled in my face, her anger causing her voice to shake. I jerked my head back and hit the wall, hard. It hurt, but I wouldn't let it show until she had descended the stairs and retreated to the kitchen.

From that point on, I learned to keep to my head down and away from the conflict between Mom and my brother.

Jonathan avoided her well and was satisfied behind the locked door to his room, content to work on his own projects and handle his own affairs. By locking that door, he not only escaped conflict with her or my father, he locked me out, too. I was collateral damage in the war they quietly waged from that day forward. His island lighthouse drifting further into the mists where voices only filter in as distorted noises easily ignored.

His lighthouse beam should have been there for me, showing me where the rocks were hidden. He should have been my ally and my hero in my search for answers. I should have been able to go to him and get the truth and be guided gently into the harbor learning the secret that my parents were keeping from me, but our mother had done too good a job of raising us. There were things you did not talk about, things that were private, even within the walls of Tooth Acre. We kept our secrets. Jonathan didn't even know I needed his help, his beam had not found me, yet.

Our bedrooms shared a wall, but we could not have lived further apart.

Eventually, my brother grew into the successful businessman my parents had always dreamed he would be. He married and had three boys of his own.

However, my brother's oldest child struggled as a teen to find his place in the world. In so many ways, I saw my own struggles in him and wished I were closer to my brother and his family so that I could be the kindred spirit my nephew needed.

One day, I was speaking with my brother's wife, who was equally frustrated with their son and my brother's lack of hands-on discipline. "He's so afraid that if we are too tough on our son, he might try to kill himself or something," she said, her hands thrown up in defeat.

Shocked into silence, I thought, *that's my fault.*

SEND IN THE CLOWNS

Two days after my attempted suicide, my "cry for help," I was summoned into the family den. It was a beautiful summer day. The den was filled with morning light, and the hum of our neighbor's lawn mower purred outside the windows, reminding me that life was moving along just fine everywhere else. I sat across from my parents' unified front on the scratchy wool plaid sofa.

My parents told me that we needed to talk. While I couldn't agree more, part of me didn't want to. I felt so stupid for the mess I had caused, and I just wanted it to go away. I didn't know how to deal with everything that was happening to me. I didn't know where to start.

We had never done this before.

Talked.

I had lived my entire life never discussing anything important with my parents outside of how I was performing in school.

So now we were supposed to be able to sit in the den and talk about "what just happened" and dig up some real emotion?

Good luck with that.

Fortunately *(unfortunately)*, I had left a note before my attempt, so we had a template of sorts.

Basically, I felt I was the fourth wheel in the family. I felt that my parents favored my brother. I believed that without me, they would have the family they wanted..

I know where the note is. I stumbled across it one day when I was in my late twenties while looking for a handkerchief for my mother to carry in her purse to a funeral we were attending. There it was in the back of the drawer. It was folded up small, like a note a schoolgirl would pass in a classroom. It was written on paper from a spiral-bound notebook, and the rough edges peeked out from the folds.

I couldn't believe it was there. It still existed. I wanted so badly to take it. I wanted to destroy it. I wanted to erase any evidence of that horrible day from the earth. I left it behind, too afraid of it and the girl who wrote it. I imagine it is still there. Mom never threw anything away. I imagine that one day I will clean out that drawer when she is no longer using it. I can deal with it then. Maybe I can love the girl who wrote it, forgive her and finally let her go.

This note, the anguished writings of a broken girl that will forever haunt me and torment my parents, also explained that I simply longed for information about who my birth mother was.

I wanted to know if they knew her. I wanted them to find out why she didn't want me.

For the first time they were honest. They didn't know who my birth mother was. I was adopted through the state, and the records were sealed.

I didn't believe them at first. I didn't trust them. Why should I? All they had ever done was lie to me about this. Lie. Lie. Lie. So I told them I didn't believe them. What did the state have to do with it?

In my naiveté, I always imaged a black-market scenario.

In my mind, a small-town doctor was looking out for his young patient. She was from a high-brow family, a socialite, a debutante. Her family would never approve of the boy she had fallen in love with. Maybe he was from the other side of town. She was scared. She had to give her baby away and keep her secret forever. She turned to this small-town doctor....

I should have known better. My parents would never do anything shady or unusual. Of course, they would follow the rules and get me through proper channels. That news hit me very hard. SEALED. How could the records be sealed? How do you unseal them?

My father was the one who talked the entire time. Mom sat by him stoically, her gaze hard on me. It was as if she didn't know who was sitting across from her.

He told me that after Mom had my brother, she couldn't have any more children, but he had always wanted a little girl.

He went on to tell me that not only were they waiting for a girl, they had turned down the first female child they were offered. She likely had a heart condition and was going to need some watching and some tests. That was too much for Mom to bear, so they passed and waited for me.

That was supposed to be the part where I felt special and wanted, I thought. *The "we didn't just have you, we CHOSE you" cliché.*

Dad told me that while I was outside being met by my Aunt Elizabeth and Jonathan, they were given a small amount of information about my birth parents.

My birth mother was from a city in upstate South Carolina. She had an affair with her boss and didn't want the baby *(ouch)* and gave me up for adoption. Her embarrassed family sent her to Charleston and the Florence Crittenton Home, which housed unwed mothers. She had me and named me Janet and surrendered me to the state. As far as they knew, she never laid eyes on me.

I was Janet. I had a name, and it was Janet.

JANET! She gave me a name, or did she? Was I named like a hurricane… Hey, what's next on the list… or was it like the dog pound. Hey, what should we call this one. How about Frisky?

*She named me Janet after her friend's older sister. She thought that girl was so beautiful, and she wanted me to have a beautiful girl's name.

Simple and straightforward. The seed of doubt that I had planted in my heart all those years earlier sprang into life again, nourished by just a little more information that could set my imagination spiraling.

An affair? An affair. He must have been older but very charming. She must have been beautiful, too beautiful to resist. Was he a married man? Was her pregnancy a complication that would ruin his well-appointed life? Maybe she never told him. Maybe she ran away. How could I find out?

I asked them why they never told me, especially when I had been asking for years.

They said they did tell me when I was very young, and I developed a stutter. They spoke to their family doctor and decided I was disturbed by this information. It was harmful for me to know, so they chose to never speak of it again.

OK, let's just stop this right here. We all know people who were adopted and spent their entire lives aware of this situation without developing a tick. So I was so traumatized by this information at a tender age that I started to randomly stutter? How on earth was this news delivered to me that it would take such an emotional toll? This should be a joyous coming together of a loving family.

"Now Elizabeth," they might have sat next to my bed, tucking me in for a cozy night's sleep. "Instead of our usual reading of 'Mr. Happy Bunny Makes a Friend,' we have decided to share some news with you." They look at each other and nod.

"You tell her, dear," my mother might have said, patting Daddy's hand anxiously.

"Well, little lady, you see, we are not your real parents. Your real mother got herself in 'the family way' and didn't want you, so she gave you away and then we decided you could live with us."

"Yes, dear," my mother would nod excitedly, "so that's why we don't really look like you or anything."

"That's exactly right, Momma!" Dad smiles proudly, "and now, here is a clown to act it all out for you in interpretive dance....Come on in Twisty."

About this time, my pacifier hits the ground, "w-w-w-w-w-wha?" and I begin screaming and crying and probably wet myself.

"Oh, dear!" they exclaim. "We will ask the doctor for his professional opinion."

Later... at the doctor's....

"Oh, I say, I say," fat Southern small-town doctor (who weirdly sounds just like Foghorn Leghorn) says, "I say, we have ourselves here a problem. You have traumatized this po'chile." I look up at him, drooling.

"Oh, doctor, what will we do now?" my parents fret.

"Not to worry. Just never speak of it again. She'll forget all about it, and everything will be fine," he tickles me under the chin avoiding the dripping spittle. "Isn't that right, little girl?"

"G-g-g-g-g-goo goo," I say.

"Oh, what a relief!" says Mom.

"But, doctor, what if she remembers and she asks about it?" Dad asks.

"For god's sake, man, LIE about it. That is the key to protecting her mental health, LIE."

This was the height of WASP behavior. Just ignore it; lie about it; and it will go away.

It was suggested that I go talk to someone about this. *Really?* That was actually good/bad news for me. I wanted help, but the catch was I didn't really know how to talk about my feelings to anyone older than me. This would be tricky. Where would we find this person?

It turned out they wanted me to see the minister at our church.

That was surprising; these very private people were going to let someone into their very private life. Looking back, that had to be a hard call for my father to make, even more for my mother. Her biggest worry was, "What will everybody think?"

I went the very next week.

SAINT PETER

It turned out that I got to speak to our youth minister, Pete Jorgenson. I already admired this man. He was the only man of the cloth that ever really made sense to me and that was appealing.

He gave a magnificent dramatic monologue in costume one Easter when I was about 12. He played the part of Judas, trying to justify his reasons for betraying Jesus to the Romans.

If I could go back in time and see my face as that small girl in the pews, I would see eyes as wide as saucers. This was my very first live theatre experience. It was amazing to me. It lit a fire in me that made me yearn to be him in that moment. To stand before an enthralled audience and move people with my words and my actions. Look at me. See me.

His monologue ended with a broken Judas grabbing his 30 pieces of silver and throwing them down in disgust and despair. I remember watching several of them rolling down the aisle and wishing one would roll as far as our pew, still the last one in the church, so I could take it and save it and never forget how I felt at that moment. Pete stepped down from the pulpit and I wanted to jump up and down and clap wildly, but you didn't do that in my church *(eyes straight ahead, young lady)* and everyone just sat in silence.

When the service was over I pushed my way through the throngs of people in their new suits and dresses and shiny white shoes to get that coin. When I arrived I was so surprised to see it was a quarter. Just a plain quarter, but for that second he had turned in into silver for me. For me, that was better than the miracles I learned about in Sunday School, this was a new kind of magic and I wanted to know how to do it.

I actually enjoyed my hour with Pete that day. I had never spoken openly with a grown-up about my feelings and actually felt understood. He sympathized with me and understood that is was OK to have the feelings I had.

"Liz, I hate to see you going through such a rough time."

Pete sat behind his desk in the church meeting rooms. His office was comfy if not a little messy. He had books. Lots of books. They were on shelves, on the floor, and on his desk. His minister's robes hung on a rolling rack in the corner.

I remembered Pete's robes the most. He never wore boring black billowy robes like the other ministers. His were all colorful and embroidered. He had robes for each season of the Christian calendar or just the seasons of the year. It was always so refreshing to see him walk in.

His bright-blue eyes smiled at me as I sat there, initially in silence, not knowing where to start and trying not to cry.

"Why do you think you are here today?" he asked.

That was a weird question.

"I'm here because I tried to hurt myself."

"Why did you do that?"

"I don't know," I shrugged. "I guess I was angry or maybe I was sad, but, basically, I just think my parents can't stand anything I do. Nothing is ever good enough for them. I'll never be as smart as my brother. They hate my friends; they think I hang with a bad crowd. They hate that I want to wear makeup. They hate this outfit!"

"Well, then, let's see if we can't figure out a way to tell them some of the things you are feeling. Maybe together, we can all open up and settle this."

I am pretty sure I rolled my eyes. I was thinking he had better have some miracle from Jesus Himself to get them to open up to me.

"First, tell me about what you feel when you think about being adopted?"

"I wonder who my birth mother is and why she gave me up. I want to know what she looks like. I wonder if she is like me. I wonder if she misses me."

"Have you considered looking for her? Have you asked your parents about helping you with this?"

"NO," I laughed nervously. "They would never do that."

"What makes you think so?"

"They say they can't. It is a sealed record and cannot be unsealed."

"Well, that's certainly true," he leaned back in his leather chair and it creaked as he looked at me. I felt like he was sizing me up. "There are adoption registries. Do you know about these?"

"No." I knew nothing.

"You could request to be added to a list, and if both the adopted child and the mother are on it, they can meet. The state has one. You could put your name on it. Who knows? She might be looking for you?"

"I was hoping she was looking for me. Do you think it could be that easy?"

"It's a start. You could go to the library and look them up."

I left, the initial feeling of happiness beginning to warm my body. This wasn't the end. Sealed, BAH! This was only the beginning. A new beginning.

My parents also saw Pete a few days later to discuss everything. I don't really know what they talked about because I never got to see Pete as a therapist again. We saw each other often at youth group and retreats, but the subject of my family life was closed as quickly as it had opened.

He always made a point to reach out to me and see how I was, but we only scratched the surface. He never got to see the homework he gave me to do, the things I had written out for him. He always looked at me as if he were a little sad. All I know is that my parents did not hear what they wanted to hear from him.

OK, your teenaged daughter downs a bottle of pills and leaves a "goodbye cruel world" note. You take her to ONE one-hour therapy session, and then you're done. Case closed. Problem solved. No need to ever again speak of it. Now go wash your hands; it's dinnertime. Really, that happened.

Many years later, Pete was my therapist once again as I struggled in an unhappy marriage. I asked him what happened that day he met with my parents, why I didn't get to come back. He couldn't give me any real answers, either because he was unsure himself or because he couldn't, ethically. He did tell me that my mother kept talking about my brother and her relationship with him, and Pete would have to bring her back to the topic of me.

Jonathan? He was a twenty-year-old dean's list college student. Sure, he was still living at home, and Mom was still doing his laundry and making his bed, but hey, this is about ME people!

He felt that they were not ready to open up or perhaps it was too difficult for them.

It hurt me to hear that more than I think he ever knew. It was as though I had been right. Maybe my mother did not know how to love her biological son and me at the same time and in the same way.

I understand most of this now. I understand that a love for a biological child is different from any love you will ever know. I understand that you cannot help the way you feel. There are many different kinds of love: Love of spouse, love of pets, love of friends and love for adopted children.

When I think about my mother now, I see that her idea of love was corrupted. Not by her hands and not her fault. She only knew what she knew. When she was growing up, she knew that her father and brothers and sisters lived a different life than she did. She knew that she was the cherished child at her grandmother's house. I'm sure Mamie felt like she had the last piece of her beloved daughter in my mother. It must have been so bittersweet for Mamie.

It must have felt terrible when she had to move back in with her family in high school, leaving the comfort of the only home and the only "mother" she had known. I wondered if she felt rejected—so much back and forth. How did her father look at her now, the object of his passion that claimed the life of his wife?

I wondered how she was received by her aunt/stepmother. I wondered about their relationship the most. Was my mother's arrival in the house an extra burden for my step-grandmother? Had they ever had a chance to form a bond? Did she see too much of her sainted sister in my mother's eyes? What was going on in that house that made my mother the woman she became? Was my mother Blackie the Cat too?

GREEN-EYED MONSTER

My teen years were full of fantasies about what my birth mother was like. I was too young to make any significant advances in my search. I was on my own again, dealing with thoughts and feelings and curiosities that I could not settle. I wrote to every adoption registry in the state of South Carolina and even a national one, submitting my name and information. And then I waited.

I fancied a woman living somewhere in South Carolina who looked exactly like me. Maybe she had other children. Maybe they looked like me, too. Of course they did; she had very strong genes, I imagined. We would all be like her. I imagined her reading to them and tucking them into bed at night. I envisioned her as the kind of mother that would hug you every time she saw you. Kisses were sweet and tenderly left on your cheeks. Praise was given with a sweet smile and encouragement enthusiastically offered when you weren't doing your best. She was beautiful and turned heads everywhere she went. Her husband and children loved her dearly.

Imagining all of these things made me jealous. I tried not to be. It wasn't my adoptive parents' fault that she didn't keep me. I would feel guilty that I was being an ungrateful child. Here I was living a fine life in a fine home with parents who provided everything for me, but my heart longed to meet another. Then I would feel like a victim, like I'm just a playing piece in the games of their lives. My birth mother makes a move, my adoptive parents take their turn and then there is me, stuck on the red square, waiting to make a move of my own. I packed all these feelings up tightly and tried to tuck them away so that they wouldn't stop me from dreaming beautiful things. It was becoming very hard to keep those weeds out of my fantasy garden. There was still that long-ago planted whisper in my ear, and it fed my jealousy and my what-ifs. Bitterness crept in and I cried a lot thinking about it. I started to doubt myself and the love my mother might still have for me. Maybe this other life had filled up her heart, and there was no room for me.

I took any opportunity I got to drive very slowly by the Florence Crittenton Home, where I was born. Sometimes I parked and simply watched the house.

I fantasized about volunteering at the Florence Crittenton Home. I would become their prized volunteer, and they would trust me with all aspects of the running of the home.

"Liz," the house mother would say, "you are such a benefit to this house. I don't know how I ever did it without you."

"Thank you, Marge. (Her name was Marge in my dream. I don't know why, it just sounded very house motherish.) You know I love my work here. Why don't you let me help you with filing and archiving? I love to organize things, and I could get in there and make it so easy for you and the rest of the staff."

"Please! Would you? Why didn't I think of that?"

"That's what I'm here for, Marge."

Eventually, I would stay late one night and break into the secret files and extract all the information I needed to discover my true identity. Yes, of course that would work.

THE MUSICAL MONTAGE MOMENT

Three days after I graduated from High School I moved out of my parents' home never to return. *Well, unless I needed money… or some food… or maybe laundry.*

When I was 19, I announced to my parents' that I was dropping out of college and marrying my boyfriend of less than a year, Jim. He was an officer in the Army and we were moving to his next station in Germany for the next four years. *Auf Wiedersehen, suckers.*

The joke was on me, I did not have the exotic life I expected full of parties and travel, I was a wife with no job and the manager of household budget. At 19, I was the youngest of all the Officers' wives and I felt the sting of their judgment.

I left my parents' home assuming I was mature enough to handle the world on my own. This was my time to blossom and grow under the ever loving and understanding glow of my young, handsome husband's affection for me.

I could not have been more wrong. I made foolish choices and struggled to find my voice in a world of grown ups who didn't quite let me in. Nothing was different for me then. If anything, things were worse. I was trapped in a foreign country and the only escape would have been to return to my parents' home full of criticism, embarrassment and judgments.

So I stayed where I was until we returned to America when I was 23 and our marriage quickly fell apart.

I didn't divorce Jim because I no longer loved him. I loved him deeply but I could not follow him on his life path anymore. I was still a young girl with no idea who I was or what I wanted to be while he was well on his way to a career. I didn't even know how to process that.

I remember the last day of our marriage. I had gone back to the town we lived in to sign our papers and to get my cat. At first, we had decided to let Big Kitty live with him, but the more we were apart, the more I needed that cat back in my life. He was a piece of my old life that I could still love and not have to leave. I remember backing out of our driveway and before I hit the street I looked back at the little house we had shared. He was still standing there, watching me leave, his hands in his pockets. Was the look on his face sadness or disappointment? I wasn't sure.

Still, I never really thought that would be the end of us. In my youthful fantasies I always imagined that we would go through our lives and have other loves and maybe even children, but that we would one day be together again.

We would be old single people who miraculously found each other again. We would marvel at each other's children and how handsome and beautiful they were. I would love his children, because I would see glimpses of my young husband in their eyes. He would love my children as his own as he fell in love with me and my spirit all over again. "Another lifetime ago" we would say and laugh holding older wrinkled hands. We would spend our golden years back in Europe. He would continue to tease me about my broken German and I would continue to roll my eyes at him and say silly American things like "oh, they know exactly what I mean.."

Now, back in the good old USA, I felt like some odd immigrant who had discovered the bounty of the new world. Opportunities and options. I felt free again. I was going to pull myself up by my bootstraps and conquer what was left of my twenties.

I moved into a little apartment back in Charleston and got the first job I could find to pay the bills. I was a cocktail waitress in a country western bar wearing short shorts and slinging draft beers at wanna be urban cowboys.

If this book was a movie, you would now be in store for a musical montage *(using some song by the likes of Carly Simon or Sheena Easton)* of Liz moving through jobs, finding husband number two and going back to college. It would end with a 26 year-old Liz graduating from college, *(success!)* buying a house with her own hard earned money *(you go girl!)* and standing in the small but neatly landscaped yard, arm around her second husband admiring her successes and wondering what the future will hold.

She dreams of big things in her future, great jobs and even bigger houses and smiles at her husband who is thinking that this is more than he ever needed and he really hopes life never changes. Liz knows she will change his mind, all good women can do that for their husbands, right? Maybe starting a family would help? *(poor misguided Liz, she is doomed, I tell you, doomed, the entire movie audience can see this, why can't LIZ?).*

THIS IS B******T

When I was 24, I was still working in the food and beverage industry in Charleston. I had left my short shorts and my beer stained cropped t-shirt at the country western bar and was now shaking martinis and muddling oranges for Manhattans at a Charleston premier four star hotel in the heart of the Historic District *(moving on up, Wheezy)* but I felt as if I was stuck in a holding pattern. I enjoyed the cold hard cash in my pockets every night, but I was watching my friends all transition into the expected young adult lifestyles that included working 9 to 5 on the weekdays and whooping it up on the weekends. I felt left out of what seemed to be a bigger picture of success and settling down.

I decided to go back to college and finish the education I had thrown away as a young, selfish nineteen-year-old girl who was still trying to find out who she was and where her life would lead her. I chose to study psychology because I knew it took crazy to know crazy, and I dreamed of helping the young teens of the world escape the depths of their confusion.

I was trying to learn to forgive my parents for the mistakes they had made, trying to understand that they did their best with the limited experience that all parents have. I was beginning to accept the fact that I might never know anything about the people who had created me, but I was still spinning my fantasy web. I was still hoping that one day some miracle would bring us together. I wasn't sure if I would ever be fully content until all the curtains were opened shining the light of truth in the dark room of my past.

What if I got to do a thesis for school on the effects of nature versus nurture. I could interview the people that work for the Child Services Bureau of South Carolina. I could get to know them. We could be good friends over my months and months of research. One night, over cocktails celebrating the success of my completed paper, I would mention my own adoption and see the sympathy in the eyes of my new friends. They cannot give me any information, they say with great regret in their eyes…but, maybe tomorrow, one of them says, you can walk by my office while I am at lunch. There might be a file on my desk that you accidentally open….

One day, a family law attorney entered my bar and changed everything. I quickly jumped, as I always did, tossed back my long curly hair, batted my pretty blue eyes at him and offered to buy him a drink if he'd answer a question for me.

"So," I leaned into him on the edge of the stainless steel bar, "what do you know about adoptions and opening sealed records?" I rested my chin on my hand, lips barely parted, awaiting the answer that my oh so smooth seduction invoked *(a girl can try, right?)*.

He suggested that I hire a private investigator to look over my Non-Identifying Information and see if there were any leads. These documents were supplied by the government on request and he insinuated that they often revealed clues that could help anyone with the right skills of deduction to put the details together and find success.

My what?

How had I not heard of this?

Apparently, it was my right to request this information from the State of South Carolina. Basically, they would send my entire case file with all the pertinent information blacked out. Just like top secret reports from the government. This was the most exciting thing I had ever heard. I immediately went about taking care of this. I requested a form that I had to fill out and notarize. Then with a measly $25 fee, I could get my report.

I actually carried around this form for months. I used the excuse that I couldn't find a notary.

Bullshit, I worked in a bar filled with attorneys.

The truth was I was terrified. What if I had been wrong all this time? What if my birth mother wasn't the woman I had fantasized about? How many times had I heard the stories that did not end well? She might not be waiting with open arms.

It was easy to spend my time deep in the fantasy world of the "what-if's." The *What-if World* had been my playground for a long time, and it was hit or miss whether it was a good place to be. If I was energized and excited, my birth mother was a charming socialite, who had always regretted her decision to give away her first-born daughter and longed for a reunion. If I was in one of my dark times, she was a victim of violence, who suffered through a pregnancy and never wanted to ever lay eyes on the product of her torturer.

I pushed those hateful thoughts aside. I couldn't let the doubts creep in because I knew deep down that she was a lovely woman. I knew she was just like me. I looked in mirrors and knew I was looking into my mother's eyes. I knew it. Didn't I?

It didn't help that my *(soon to be ex)* second husband wasn't exactly supportive. I knew he was concerned I would be disappointed, and I let that feed my doubts, the weeds once again choking the garden of hope inside me.

It was my best girlfriends that pushed me to see it through. We had all spent so many hours discussing it. They knew how much I longed for answers. We were all getting older and thinking about someday having families of our own, so the thoughts of family hit closer to our hearts than they ever had before.

Of course, they wanted me to follow through. It was curiosity, wasn't it? Nothing would change in their lives. They were not running the risk of rejection.

Nonetheless, the deed was finally *fait accompli*. I approached the mailbox, filled with nervous excitement tinged with just enough fear to make my hands shake, and I mailed one of the most important letters in my life.

And then I waited.

After about a month, I wasn't running to the mailbox every day. The disappointment was too much to bear daily, so I all but gave up. The watched pot never boiled.

On a hot summer Saturday, I went for a power walk with my dog, Rudy. We rounded the comer to my block when the mailbox caught my eye. The flap was left open because a large manila envelope had exceeded its capacity and was jutting out.

Just like that, it was there.

I didn't even make it into the house before I was ripping open the envelope and spilling its contents onto my sweaty lap.

I was prepared, to some extent, to see the blackouts that were prominent on page one. All names, cities, occupations, or any distinguishing features would be covered with whiteout tape before being copied. I knew this.

Page One:

```
Worker: ******************

Abstract for: Janet

Mother: 20, HS and 2 yrs. Coll., Sales Clerk —
gifts and accessories, 5'6, 125, brn, blue, f.
Intelligent, good grades, plays piano and sings,
plays basketball and tennis, dances, art courses,
ceramics, likes sewing, swims, seems mature, very
attractive looking, well-liked in home, high
standards.
```

I must have read that over and over. I wanted to memorize it. I wanted to think about every word that Worker ******** had used to describe my mother. In many ways, she had just described me. I was everything that they said about her. Same height, weight, complexion, eye color... the piano? The singing? I even gave myself the "very attractive looking" nod because that made me more like HER.

High standards. I knew what they meant. She was accustomed to a certain lifestyle. It's as I thought, the society girl had gotten herself into trouble. I knew it!

And then the description of my father:

```
AF: (What's the A for? I found out it was for "alleged") 26, HS and
4 years college, Salesman, 5'11, 175, brn, hazel,
c. Seems very intelligent, good personality, nice
looking, good mixer, successful.
```

Twenty-six was a young boss, if my father's story was true. I began to buy into the seduction of my poor younger mother by this nice-looking good mixer. I could see how he had cast his spell over her.

Maybe everyday she would come to work, and he would be there with his dazzling smile and smooth talk (that good mixer). They would flirt over the jewelry counter. He would just happen to be around when she took her break, asking her questions about her day or what she might be doing later that evening.

Would she come to work every day looking forward to seeing him? Would she often catch him looking at her from across the room? Maybe they would stand a little too close to each other in the back room. Perhaps he would steal their first kiss right there, away from the prying eyes of the other girls on the showroom floor. She would return blushing and a little frazzled. The other girls would know this was going on. They might even be jealous. How long before he asked her out? How long did they keep it a secret?

All this and I was only on page one. A magnificent story was waiting to be discovered on page two. All the things I ever wanted to know were here in my hands for the first time. I was twenty-seven-years-old, and the mysteries were finally about to be revealed to me. I just knew I would find the answers on these pages.

I was still sitting on the steps to my house. The sun was warm on my face, and my dog was lying, panting at my feet, looking up at me with his happy doggy face.

I took a moment to enjoy the last moments of living in darkness and took a deep breath before continuing. *Here I come Page Two. Let me have it!*

My first thought: the good people at the Children's Bureau of South Carolina really needed to invest in a new copy machine. I had in my hands a badly copied, black-streaked page with a dark stripe down the middle, making it very difficult to read. That wouldn't have been so bad. I could have handled that. What hit me like a fast kick to the stomach was the amount of words that had been redacted. It was going to be hard enough, but wow.

******* Baby Case

This case was referred to the Children's Bureau

```
of South Carolina by Mrs. ********* of the
************* in ************** and accepted by
Mrs. *****************
**********  I  talked  with  ********  at  the
*********** on this date. ****** had entered the
Home ********* in 1967 and her hospital name is
****. *****'s mother brought her to the home and
when I asked where her father ************** was
she said he could not leave work. ****'s parents
are Mr. ******** and Mrs. ******** of ********.
Mr. ******* is a sales manager at ******** they
manufacture ********** equipment. Mrs. ********
does not work outside the home.
```

They continue to describe some siblings and even a close relative who was also expecting a child at the same time as my mother.

It was hard to wrap my brain around it. It made me stop and start reading over and over, wanting it to flow and fill me up. Instead it was frustrating and made me feel lost.

My emotions were all over the place. Here she was, in a terrifying situation. Her relative was pregnant at the same time? Interesting. That had to make it harder for her, seeing her family enjoying the arrival of a new member while she hides her own pregnancy as a dark secret. Who had she confided in? Who was helping her? I could only hope she was not dealing with all of these feelings alone. What was I going to find out?

Nonetheless, I had to keep going. The words had definitely been well blocked out with whiteout tape, but it had been a big job for the secretary. What were the odds that she hit every mark? If she could have just accidentally left ONE CLUE. ONE piece of tape unstuck or, better yet, not stuck well enough, and it shifted and moved while it was run through the worst copy machine in the entire State of South Carolina. *I bet the prisons have nicer machines than this one.* This left just enough hope for me to slow down and devour every word very carefully.

My mother had entered the home in December, but it seemed as though the social worker did not interview her until February 1. That had to have been unsettling for her, all alone in a strange city in a strange place without her family. The report said she had three roommates. Were these girls like her? Were they nice to her? Did they confide in one another or try not to to look too closely at each other for fear they will know somebody who knows them and the secrets will be exposed?

There was some mix-up that caused her case to be overlooked, and now they were in a hurry. The baby was due on or around February 17, and they needed to do lots of work to make plans for her baby.

The first paragraph was all about her. When and where she was born (blacked out, of course, with the exception of the year). It did give me the year she graduated from high school, 1966, so I was grateful for that nugget of information. She didn't explain why she only went to college for a short time, but she did talk about her job, which she loved. (I noticed that here they had blacked out the kind of store it was, but I know from the abstract that it was something like a gift shop, so I sensed this was my first crack in the case.)

`A **** store, and she planned to make this her profession.`

AH HA! Plan number one, call a gift shop in her hometown, any one will do, and ask which one was open in 1967 and hope it still is …. easy, got it. This is the South. It could be closed ten years but folks will still talk about it and even use it as a reference. You cannot get directions to any place in town from a Southerner without them using a reference to a building or shop that is long gone.

Example:

"Excuse me," an out of towner will ask a local southern man, "I am trying to get to the bank but I am lost."

"Well now," he approaches their car window wiping his brow with a red bandana, "that's just a piece down the road. You head on up yonder to the red light by the Old Wal Mart and turn left and it's just a hop skip and jump on down on the left by the gas station, but actually that used to be a barber shop when I was a boy and good lord, Ole man Causey kept that place hopping. He served lemonade in the summer and I remember just going down there to get some with my friend Little Kenny, we called him

Little Kenny because his Daddy was Big Kenny…"

They continued to talk about how well she was doing in the home and how everyone liked her. She showed some ceramic pieces she was making in the arts class. She also learned to make fried chicken. She said she finally felt very relaxed there, knowing she could just wait for the baby and not worry about anyone finding out.

They inquired about my father, and she told them that she would rather not say who he was other than she knew him well enough to supply any information they might need. The report said she seemed puzzled that they would expect to talk to him about it. She insisted that he did not know, and she wanted to keep it that way. He believed that *****'s family had sent her for a vacation with her best friend. She anticipated returning and resuming the relationship, and it was too late to tell him now.

My mother, *******, had many questions for the social worker. She was very concerned about what would happen to the baby and wanted to know about the kind of home it would be placed in. The worker assured her that they worked within the girl's wants to help place the baby. This made ***** very happy.

In the caseworker's evaluation, she mentioned how attractive ***** was. She said that ****** spoke highly of her close-knit family. ***** was from an above-average socioeconomic family, and her clothes were quite distinctive.

The social worker felt that over time, she would loosen ***** up a bit more and that ***** would feel more comfortable naming the father of the child. ***** spoke freely about him, although she was still not naming him.

In the next interview ***** named the father as ****** ******* but had decided it would not do to tell him about the pregnancy. She regretted not telling her boyfriend and parents about their baby right away. She felt certain he would have married her and that her parents would have wanted her to keep the baby. She was afraid she had now waited too long and didn't want to bring shame to her and his families. Her father, *********, held a very important position at the ********** and this would disgrace him. Now, though, she had left town under false pretenses and returning with a baby would have given "everybody a lot to say." She was happy to say that he still stopped by her parent's home to ask about her and see if she was "having a big time" on her vacation. She thought that if there was any chance of continuing the relationship, he must never know.

The housemother was interviewed at this juncture in the case and described my mother, *****, as refined, elegant, and polished.

The next interview with ****** had her giving background information on her parents. Where they were from, the sizes of their families, and the age her grandparents were. It was a hard paragraph to read because every other word seemed to be a ********. As I carefully read along, an actual name popped out at me. Jill. *****'s hospital name was Jill. They chose an alias upon arrival and this was hers. *JILL. I think this will come in very handy when I get my dream volunteer job at the unwed mothers home and break into the secret files.*

Next entry:

    2-29-68: ****************** baby born at the
    ************** in Charleston on this date. The
    baby was a girl weighing 7lbs 12 and ? oz. She was
    pronounced in good physical condition.

    ******** returned to the home the next day. The
    caseworker arrived to have her sign the agreement
    to have the baby removed from the hospital and
    sent to the temporary home. She found my mother
    tired and weepy. ***** signed the form.

The next entry was March 12. The caseworker returned to find my mother in much better spirits and looking very attractive. *This was the caseworker's favorite word.* She was so grateful for the help and care she received. She said her parents were preparing everyone for her return home. She had been sunning herself outside because she was supposed to be away on vacation and should return tanned and healthy looking. She made a point of telling her caseworker that when she returned she would inform her boyfriend that she would not be having sex again unless she was married and if he were to break up with her over that, she was OK with his choice.

The next entry:

> Surrender: ***** and I then discussed the surrender of her baby and she understood that she was giving up all rights and claims to the baby and that she would be placed in a suitable home as quickly as possible. ***** filled in and signed the surrender form which was witnessed by Mrs. *****. She cried a great deal during this time and I felt that all of her pinned up feelings were coming through and at last she had faced up to really what she had done.
>
> Evaluation: I feel that ***** is a very intelligent mature type girl who is quite polished and accomplished in so many ways. She seems to be from people who are very high in socioeconomic standards. The information on the alleged father was verified and I believe this baby has very good potential and would fit nicely into any home the Bureau might select for her. ******** 5-24-68.

The rest of the report was the case about my placement and the *******s had stopped. This was a relief and it was very interesting to see another person's take on the first months of my life with the Butlers.

It began with that hot summer day in August. A six month old Janet was soon to become Elizabeth.

I already knew that the first people to meet me were my brother and aunt, and now I knew that the first parent to hold me was my father. They described him as being charmed by the lovely baby and that I took to him readily. The caseworker left me alone in the room with them so they could look me over and discuss things, but she said they were out in "half a minute," so pleased with the child and ready to move on with the process. Jonathan came to the room at this time and he was described as "one of the most enthusiastic little boys I have ever seen about a new member of the family. The worker feels this placement went well."

Worker ******** called and visited the Butlers regularly over the next year. She had friends in Mount Pleasant, and they all knew the story of the beautiful baby the dentist, Dr. Butler, and his wife had adopted. I was all the talk in tiny Mount Pleasant. My mother worried about all the company she was getting, and she commented that she hoped it would be back to normal soon. I'm sure my mother wasn't thrilled with all the attention, but she managed it well, it seems.

Many years later, my father gave me the written correspondence that they had to provide to the state over the first year of the adoption regarding

My Non- Identifying Information

my well-being and how I was getting along. Of course, the good doctor had to have a copy for his own records and they were carefully written on copy paper. Of the twelve that were written, only one came from my mother, he would have wanted to handle it all. My proud father documenting in his doctor/scientific way all the progress I was making, calling me The Queen of Hearts and in every one you knew exactly how many teeth I had.

The last line of the report read.

    It appears that this placement is going well.

AND UNTO HER A CHILD IS BORN

My longing for finding my biological mother and family increased more and more as I grew older and more independent of the household that raised me, but never so much as when the dreaded biological clock sounded its alarm in my soul. I was probably ordering a second *(third)* scotch and soda and lighting a cigarette when it went off. I tried to hit the snooze button *(fourth scotch, hey mister, do you have light?)*, but it wouldn't leave me alone. I was 28 years-old, and I discovered I wanted a baby of my own.

I did not have an easy time getting pregnant. First, I had to convince my husband to let me. I asked almost everyday for months. At first it was subtle.

"So, this would make a nice baby's room wouldn't it"

"Do you think a baby would get all my curly hair?"

"I wonder what kind of mother I would be?"

And then I got more aggressive.

"If I don't ever have a baby of my own it will haunt me for the rest of my life and THAT, Mr. Man, will be all your fault!"

He finally caved.

Then, I had to actually make one.

That shouldn't be too hard, abandon all forms of birth control and schedule romantic and seductive evenings on exactly the 12th, 13th and 14th days of my cycle. Perfect.

That didn't work. The months passed with no positive results.

So I added the 11th and the 15th day too and after several anxiety-producing months I had the only husband in the tri-state area that cried after sex.

I was in total shock. I wanted this and I was ready so why wasn't it happening?

Primarily, my life was charmed and I got the things I wanted and worked for. I got the boys I liked, I got into the college I wanted, I got the jobs I wanted and needed to make a living, if I went shopping I scored the CUTEST outfits… things had often gone well for me. Jealous yet? Hold onto that thought.

The one thing I wanted. The one thing I would have traded my many blessings to have was a biological connection, whether that be my birth mother or a child of my own. The thing most everyone I knew had and never gave a second thought.

It made me very sad every month when I had, yet again, failed. I turned to my mother to share in this sadness, thinking this was another chance for us to bond. The hope for a child of your own is a strong one. I wondered how long she had cried at the monthly reminder that she had failed to conceive. How long before adoption was discussed? Was it her idea or was it Daddy's? Did he see the sadness in her and offer a solution to please his wife? Did Mom simply give up? I longed to talk to her about it and share in this important opportunity to connect.

"I just can't seem to get over the sadness every time," I shared. "All I see are pregnant women and babies everywhere I go. Was that what it was like for you?"

"Was what like?" she asked, clearing off the dishes from the lunch we had shared with Daddy, just like old times.

"Not being able to get pregnant."

She straightened up immediately and looked at me as if I had just insulted her to the core, "I could most certainly have had all the children I wanted!"

"Wait, then why did you adopt me? I thought Dad said…."

"Elizabeth, I was not going to do that again. It was the most unpleasant thing I had ever done! I can remember telling the doctor that I just wanted to go home and have this over with." She turned her back to me and faced the sink.

"So," I was so confused at this point, "when did you decide to adopt?"

"Elizabeth, I don't know. That was Daddy's decision, ask him."

Sting. Bonding opportunity crashed and burned.

Conversation over.

When my daughter, Daphne, was born twenty days before my thirty-first birthday, her birth filled up so many holes in my heart that nothing else ever could. Little pink spackle covering the dents and scuffs, smoothing things over for a new shiny coat of love. Her tiny spirit poured into my soul and filled the empty places with effervescence. She was delivered by emergency cesarean section, and I only got a glimpse of her before she was whisked out of the room.

The wait to get her back was the most prolonged agony of my life. Where was my baby? What were they doing that was taking so long? I had to hold her. I wanted to look deeply into her eyes. I needed her. My arms were emptier than they had ever been. No one could console me. I felt myself getting angry. I snapped at everyone who didn't understand

Daphne age 6 and me, even our sunburns are matching

my anxiety. The baby is fine, they would tell me. "I KNOW she is fine!" I exclaimed. "I just want her back now. Bring her back."

It was then I realized that my heart ached for my birth mother. She must have gone through the very same thing—the baby taken quickly from the room, nurses with hushed voices. I couldn't imagine the pain she must have felt to just let her daughter go. She never even saw me? Was anyone there to comfort her?

I've never felt such relief as when my daughter arrived all tightly swaddled and pink. I had a daughter of my own, with my blue eyes and downy curly hair. She looked at me, and for the first time in my life, I looked back at somebody I was related to. She was blood of my blood and flesh of my flesh. It was a miracle. I had so much love for this little creature in my arms. I didn't want her out of my sight. I was anxious every time someone else tried to hold her.

If there is a God, and I think there is, he sent me the most wonderful answer to my prayers. It was as though he saw my sadness and my craving to be like someone else, to have the same face as someone else, and he gave me a sweet little doppelganger.

As soon as she was born I was aching for another. I couldn't stand the thought of her being an only child. She needed a brother or a sister.

It took some convincing with my husband who was content with our threesome but her sweet brother, Aidan, quickly followed her birth. Here was another child who looked so much like me. Another chunky little gift from my body to admire. I said things like, "he has my eyes" and "look, those are my toes."

I was going to fill up my family and create these little Lizes so that I could see DNA work. When they were grown, I could send them all over the State of South Carolina. One day, some stranger would stop them. "Why," they would say, "You look exactly like (insert name of my birth mother here). I must lead you to her!!"

We will be a team of blue-eyed truth seekers using our powers for good. Our mission: fight injustice, right that which is wrong, and serve all mankind... or is that just the Super Friends?

SIX MONTHS OLD

I often wondered about this gap of time between my birth and my placement with my parents. Six months seemed like such a long time to me.

At first, I liked to soothe myself with the idea that she must have tried to keep me!

She saw the baby and screamed to be reunited. "Call it off!" she would demand and the baby would be given back to her, nurses exchanging nervous glances with each other wondering if this was the right thing to do. My beautiful mother, sweat plastering her dark hair to her forehead, would hold me closely and coo over her daughter.

The doctor would be called back in. "You have to speak with her," the concerned nurse's voice whisper as they hurried back to the delivery room, their soft soled shoes padding down the shiny tile floor of the brightly lit hospital hallway.

The doctor is not successful in his attempts, the new mother strong with emotions and possessiveness clings to her newborn.

My last hope of that dream was extinguished by the report I had just gotten. She never even saw me. But who did? Who took this tiny baby and sacrificed sleep and freedom to care for me. Who rocked me to sleep and tucked me in. Who sang lullabies to me. Who dressed me in the pink smocked dress I met the Butler's in? Who kissed my chubby cheek one last time?

Did I love that woman? Did I cry when they took me away from her? Did my fat arms reach out and did I twist and turn in the caseworker's arms, trying to see her face until they drove me away?

With all four of my children, I looked at them very closely the day they turned 6 months old. By then, they could sit up. They watched my every move as I drifted around them during our day to day routines. When I entered a room they could look up and see me, huge smiles of recognition and joy covering their sweet faces. If something startled them they grabbed for me, trusting that I was there for them. If they were tired they reached for me, knowing I would comfort them.

Was there any separation anxiety for me? Was it easy for me to trust this new family and feel safe in their arms? How long did it take?

There is a picture of me at my new home where I lived in Mount Pleasant. I am about to be proudly toted about town to meet my new family. I am sitting on my new mother's lap, my arm stretched out to it's fullest length holding her at bay, my face serious as I stare a hole right through the camera. Was this how it was for me or was I just caught in a moment, as a typical little baby unwilling to bend to the wishes of her first (?) photographer.

Was I a difficult child to bond with? Was I scared and shy at first? Is this why we never had the bond I so often longed for? Was it my fault?

Sometime in the first few days as Elizabeth Butler, 6 months old.

**My first daughter, Daphne, at 6 months old reacting to
my entrance into the room**

THE BI-LO EFFECT

I don't think my mother has ever completely forgiven me for being, in her opinion, a difficult child to raise. It's not like I was obstinate or lazy. Quite the opposite; I was loud and demonstrative with my emotions. *Funny how part of that word is "demon."* My elaborate excuses for unsavory behaviors or dramatic interpretations of why I needed some attention from her began to work on one of her last nerves. *If you take HER word for it.*

For her, raising a child meant not having to hear from it all that often. I was not gifted with the ability to suppress my feelings. They poured out all over the house and ruined her idea of the perfect family. It felt like I added aggravation to her perfectly ordered world. It's really no wonder that she favored my brother, and as an outcome, he has mastered the art of living a life that no one in the family actually knows anything about.

Mom and I do our best talking on the phone. It's not easy going over to her house to see her. All of my bad memories are tainted with the smells of her home. Eucalyptus, the faint smell of mold, Yankee Candle, and sadness. I walk in the front door and am bombarded with memories. I know she feels this as well. So walls go up and old patterns repeat themselves.

I don't think my mother is happy unless she is complaining. Any good news is received with immediate rejection of perfect bliss. Vacations: too expensive. Leading role in the latest play: so many lines to memorize. Another child on the way: oh dear, again? If you tried to convince her of the happiness she should be sharing with you she would respond, "Well, anyway." That is "Katherine Butler" for "we are done with this conversation."

Some people see the glass half full and some see it half empty. My mother's glass was always full... of something she didn't like.

As my mother aged, I took her to her doctor's appointments. As we went from one new specialist to the next, there was always an abundance of forms to fill out. My favorite was "Person To Be Contacted In Case of Emergency."

"Put down Jonathan," Mom said, looking through her pocketbook to grab a wilted handkerchief to dab her watery eyes.

"Jonathan? You are kidding me, right? Do you see him anywhere, Mom? I'm here right now, what the hell?"

"Well, anyway."

She sent me to the Bi-Lo to fill her prescriptions now that driving was not easy anymore.

"You are Katherine Butler's daughter?" the girl behind the counter brightly asked.

The pharmacist stopped his careful inventory of the back to come around the aisle and smile at me. "Oh we just love Katherine. She is the dearest lady. You've got one wonderful mother. Always so sweet and kind. You are so lucky."

I often wondered if they saw the confusion on my face. Did it slip out behind the facade of good Southern daughter?

"Thank you, she is very sweet." I say the words. I know they are true, I just want some more of it for ME.

Mom's Parkinson's disease not only robbed her of her ability to drive, it also left her unable to cook. I decided that I needed to devote a few days a week to running her around and helping prepare meals that she could easily serve herself throughout the day.

That was a big undertaking. I was just about to open a new business, but I put this on hold. Once again, the opportunity to bond with my mother had arisen, and if we didn't get this right now, we were running out of time.

We started right away. I went to her house on certain mornings, and she always had a list of things she would like to do and places she would like to shop, ending, as always, with the Bi-Lo.

We would arrive at our location, and I would help her from the car.

We got a cart she could lean on or I grabbed her cane from the back of the car so that she wouldn't tire out too quickly. We entered our locations, her "haunts" she called them, and most of the salespeople recognized her right away.

"Miss Katherine," they'd say, "don't you look good today. I'm so glad to see you."

Mom thanked them, exchanged niceties, and we walked away.

I was never introduced. I might as well have been the hired help. It started to bother me, so I said something as we walked away from one of the salespeople.

I mimicked Mom's Southern accent, "And this is my lovely daughter, Elizabeth. Isn't she just the sweetest little ole' thing to carry me all over creation?"

"Well, anyway," she said looking right ahead.

We made our way to the garden store, her favorite. My mother spent her entire life creating the most beautiful yards and gardens around her home. She even won awards for her hard work. Until her disease completely robbed her of the one thing she loved more than anything— her yard. She insisted on shopping for it and maintaining it.

She spent a small fortune trying to save her precious yard through the years. She hired a man who wandered the neighborhood looking for yard work to do for cash.

"I don't know what I would have done without that colored man helping me," she said.

"Oh my god, Mom, what color is he?"

"Elizabeth, he's black."

"You could just say that, Mom. We don't say colored anymore."

"Well, anyway, I can't do a thing without him. He's my best friend."

"Mom, he's really not your best friend. You are paying him for all this work; he's not just stopping by to visit."

On this particular day, as we wandered through the garden department, the manager immediately spotted her and hurried over to speak with one of his favorite customers. They were so happy to see one another as they chatted about the latest pretty bloomer or the latest annoying blight. Finally he looked at me and introduced himself.

"I'm so sorry, I'm Andy. Miss Katherine has been a valued customer here for years. We just love our gardens and our little visits don't we, Miss Katherine."

"We sure do." She smiled coyly. *Was she flirting?*

"That's wonderful, Andy," I said, taking his strong and calloused hand in mine, thrilled to finally be noticed. "I'm Liz Duren. I'm her daughter."

His eyebrows rose, momentarily disappearing into his hairline. "Daughter?" he asked, glancing at Mom and back at me, "I didn't know she had a daughter." He turned his inquisitive eyes back to mom. "You have a son, though, right?"

The next week, I called Mom at our usual time on Monday morning to discuss her plans.

"Oh, Elizabeth, I'm going to have to call you back. I have someone at the house right now."

"Oh, sure, no problem, " I said. "Who's there?"

"I am interviewing a girl that's going to start driving me around and helping me run my errands and cook for me," she stated plainly and very matter of factly.

"Well, anyway."

I KNEW IT

I read my Non-Identifying Information over and over the day it arrived. I felt happy and sad. I felt exhilaration and rage. I laughed and I cried. I called several friends to let them know the results, carefully reading sections to them. I couldn't contain my feelings. I was finally justified and knew that everything I had felt about my birth mother deep down was true.

She did look like me. I knew it.

She was everything my happy heart had imagined her to be. I knew it.

I felt her pain for the loss of the baby she had given up and then immediately questioned my feelings. WAS she sorry? The report said that she cried a lot. Did she think about it? How often did it come to mind? How long before February 29 would come and go and she wouldn't even notice? There was so much to think about. So much that needed to be investigated and solved.

Over the next year, and through many bottles of wine, my best friend, Vicki, and I became experts at carefully evaluating every word of this document. It was our Rosetta Stone to the truth. We even learned to count the size of the blocked out letters based on the typewriter spaces below them.

We knew she had a six-letter first name. We saw the bottom of a letter peeking out from under the tape and that gave us more clues.. We were sure, now, where she was from...part of the name was clearly peeking out under another piece of tape. She mentioned the family had a ***** home on **************. We deciphered that those fifteen spaces could spell out Isle of Palms or Pawley's Island... Ah ha! We were learning more and more.

We deduced that the gift shop had to be Zeigler's. It was a family owned store that had been a part of her hometown for many years.

We called Zeigler's. *Hello, my name is Liz and I am calling from Charleston.* We told the nice man who answered the phone that we were long-lost family members hoping to create a family tree. We had heard tell of a cousin of his but we were not sure of her name. We DID know that she had been a tad of a scandal to the family. She had a child out of wedlock. You might remember who this is and help us get in touch with the family we never knew.

The man I spoke to on the phone had been there for a long time, but he wasn't the owner in 1967 or 1968, and he couldn't begin to know who it was we were looking for as they had many different girls working there. I left my number, just in case.

I also turned to an interesting piece of evidence in the report concerning my alleged father. His father's occupation was listed as fire chief. We figured that leaving that occupation uncovered had to be a big mistake in the report.

I often wondered if the woman standing at this subpar xerox machine ever left little clues for me on purpose. Maybe she sympathized with the people who asked for this information and thought, "Oh, what can it hurt if I throw them a tiny bone?"

Not only did we have his job title, we had a description. He was a striking 6'3" tall. There could only be one fire chief in her hometown, right? We immediately started to call 411, looking for the fire department non-emergency numbers. *Where was GOOGLE when you really needed it! It would be years before we had that to help us.*

We filled our glasses with red wine courage and sat on Vicki's couch, trying to decide what to say. How would we pull this information out of some stranger? We decided to pretend that we were throwing a surprise family reunion for my elderly father. We wanted to get in touch with a branch of his family that he hadn't seen in awhile. We just knew this "cousin" was a tall fire chief in 1968. Would you know who this statuesque fellow was?

I practiced my best upstate accent on Vicki. We giggled and high fived, and the call was placed.

Hello, my name is Liz and I am calling from Charleston.

The man who answered the phone was too young to remember anyone like that, so the phone was passed around the room until we got an older fellow who thought he could help us.

"Now, that sounds like Jimmy Conway," he said. *I imagined this older man sitting at an aluminum dinner table eating a bowl of fireman chili and flipping through a girly magazine waiting for the piercing sound of the fire alarm to rouse him to duty.* "He's an old timer, alright, and I wanna say that man topped over 6 feet."

"That's amazing! Hey, I hate to be trouble, but you don't have a local phone book, do you? I'm calling from Charleston."

We hung up with a phone number and what we thought was our first big break. I could soon be talking to my grandfather.

An elderly man answered my call that night, sitting in the comfort of his home.

"Hello, am I speaking to Chief Conway?"

"Well, yes, ma'am you sure are!" He sounded so sweet and upbeat. Vicki sat next to me on her sofa. She was anxious for me, clutching her glass of wine, nodding, and encouraging me to keep going.

"Well, you don't know me. My name is Liz, and I'm calling from Charleston." my heart is beating wildly in my chest.

"Charleston, my wife and I love to see Charleston."

"Yes, sir, it sure is pretty. I'm so sorry to bother you this evening, but I have the most unusual question to ask you. If you are the fellow I'm looking for, you would have had a son who was about 26 or 27 in 1968." I scooted closer to Vicki and held the phone out from my ear so that we could both listen. I was nervous and excited.

"Oh, now, I'm sorry you do have the wrong person. My wife and I could never have any children."

"Oh," I deflate. Vicki slumps back on the couch in frustration. "I'm sorry to hear that."

"Well, that was long time ago, young lady. It's nothing to be sorry about now. Let me ask you, what made you call me? How did you get my name?"

"I'll tell you the truth," I said with nothing to lose. "I am an adopted child. I have very little information on my birth parents, but I do know that my grandfather would have been a 6'3" fire chief in 1968 or there about."

"Is that so?" He pondered the words I had just spoken as we sat in a brief silence.

"You wouldn't happen to know who I'm talking about from 1968, would you?" I asked with the last bit of hope I had for this phone call.

"I'm sorry, young lady, I don't know how I can help you." Another long silence, "I tell you what, though, you sound like a sweet girl and I hope you find what you are looking for."

"I do too. It's not all that easy," I said.

He laughed, "No, I imagine it isn't, but it sure would have been somethin' else to find out I had a long-lost granddaughter out there looking for me. That would sure have been somethin'."

Many years later, I found out that that one clue in my report should have cracked this case wide open. Jimmy Conway knew exactly who I was talking about. He was keeping a secret. It was a long time before I knew that he was not just protecting his fellow fireman, he was protecting me from a secret that he must have thought I would not have handled very well back then. A tragedy within the family. A secret I still keep.

Our dashed hopes turned to visions of driving upstate and doing some Cagney-and-Lacey-style detective work, but there was always something. Work. Family things.

My *(soon-to-be-ex)* second husband was still completely against our investigation and was not at all thrilled with the idea of my going any further down this road. He reminded me that no one had ever come looking for me in all these years, so what made me think my birth mother wanted to hear from me?

Ouch. This was an awful thing to say to my naturally insecure self, and I let it almost completely extinguish the fire of hope that I had carried around for so long. *Almost.*

ROAD TRIP

I decided to take out a personal ad in newspapers across the state. Not knowing where my birth mother might be living now, I thought she might see my ad and contact me. The ad ran for a month, only on weekends. It read:

Are you my mother?

"I was born in Charleston, SC on February 29, 1968 and put up for adoption. I would like to meet you on your terms and with respect to your privacy."

I listed a post office box for my address and I checked the box daily. I got exactly two letters. One was from the son of a woman who had given up a child in Charleston around that time. The dates were not right and the details didn't really match up. Not my mother. The other was from an inmate at our maximum security prison who thought maybe we could start writing letters and could I send him a picture and maybe we could have sex one day. *Definitely not my mother.*

Nothing ever came of my personal ad, and I let my post office box rental expire along with my hopes.

I joined a local mothers group. We would get together several times a week to let our children play. This was such a fun time for me and the kids, and it was delightful to have support from women with children the same ages as mine. I found myself once again telling my story to new friends and a new audience. It was the easy segue from, "Look how much your children look like you! Who do you all take after? Your mother or father?"

It always seemed that when a new group of people heard this story, they all got swept up in the excitement of helping me look for my mother. Everyone thought he or she had something to contribute, but one really did. Carol was fascinated by my tale, and by this point I had so much to add—the documents and the story behind them.

Carol told me that she was from the upstate, and she knew the high school my mother probably attended and even a popular, fancy gift shop that had been around since the 1950's. She would be happy to go with me one day and help me get around.

The road trip was planned. I spent the entire night before so excited I could barely sleep. I devoted my insomnia to making 80's mix playlists for the car's CD player. We were so full of enthusiasm and excitement. Nervous laughter and *what-if* conversations filled the three-hour drive. The drive for answers! We were so naive that we had no idea of the scope of what could lie before us. We didn't care. We were full of the love of the chase.

Our first stop: the high school.

Our plan was painfully simple. Get the yearbook from 1966, my birth mother's senior year, and look at every picture until we found the girl that looked just like me. *How hard could that be?* Surely her image would jump off the page. We would we done by lunch!

Even the school librarian got swept up in our frenzy. She led us to a private room with a copy machine and the yearbook and eagerly offered to help. It was a large graduating class, and the task ended up being rather daunting. By the "H's," we were thinking that this wasn't going to be as easy as we had hoped. Our enthusiasm dimmed, but only a little.

There were plenty of girls that might, a little bit, maybe, look like me. Our task was made more difficult because the photos were black and white. This was going to require more time and effort than we actually had, so we decided to Xerox every page for future reference. We limited our copies to only the pages with possible candidates because the machine took nickels, and we only had so many. Only brunettes would do.

I decided that the list of senior superlatives would help us for several reasons. I had been a senior superlative *(most talented, thank you)* and perhaps she was one. Also, I couldn't help but think that if any of the women in all of the high school had gotten themselves pregnant just years after graduation, the girl voted "Most Popular" probably knew who it was. Good gossip like that wasn't going to slip past Miss Popular's pretty little ears, now would it?

I also checked out the back of the yearbook for the ads section.

Maybe some candid shot back there would have captured her in a relaxed moment laughing with friends, books clutched to her chest, wearing a PINK LADIES jacket.

It was there that I hit what I thought was the jackpot. On page 120 was a quarter-page ad for Zeigler's Fine Gifts, and in it was a photograph of a young brunette working behind the counter, smiling and pretending to be showing a customer something.

We were floored. This could be her! Could we be lucky enough to have found her on our first stop? We squealed with delight and jumped up and down with pleasure. This precious Xerox copy was taken to our second stop.

Stop Number 2: Zeigler's Fine Gifts.

We discovered the most charming little downtown. Zeigler's was one of the shops lining the main street, so we walked in with our Xerox copy in hand. Inside were displays of beautiful china, shelves of exquisite porcelain and glass cases filled with very expensive jewelry. I imagined how much fun this job must have been for my birth mother, working around all these pretty pieces. I pictured her gazing over the engagement ring case, wondering which one might be hers one day.

Then it hit me.

"Carol," I reached for her hand, "my mother has been here. She touched that door; she stood on this very spot. This is the first time in my life when I know I am somewhere she has been."

"Oh, Liz," she said, squeezing my hand, "you say it like she was just here ten minutes ago."

As far as I was concerned, it could have been. That's how close I felt to finding her. I knew that at any minute I would feel her like a cool mist that brushes past you on a warm summer day.

We asked for the manager and explained our unusual mission to him. We tried to be as delicate as possible. This town might be as close a community as Charleston, and while we were desperate for information, we did not want people on their guard. We stuck to my usual ruse; that we were researching a family tree and had a mystery relative we would love to connect with.

The manager took one look at the picture and said he was sure he knew who the girl was. She was still living in the town and had married. He gave us her name. HER NAME.

Score.

Full of nervous energy and excitement, Carol and I talked about our next move over lunch. What should we do with this information? It was a long shot, but hadn't we come all this way to take every chance we could? What if we were right? What if we called her and she was so happy to hear from me that she insisted we come over immediately and meet—to have the reunion I had dreamed of. The long, tight hug. The tears. The long-awaited acceptance.

We see each other for the first time. Our eyes lock, and we stand frozen for just a moment, taking each other in, noticing the similarities. Feeling the emotion that has brought us to the same place and the same time, we both tear up, and then she reaches her arms out to hug me. We cry. The hug lasts a long time. When we finally pull apart, we look at each other again and laugh. How happy we are to be together and oh, now what a mess we are, all these tears. She takes my hand and leads me to the sofa and hands me a tissue. She tells me how happy she is to see me and how long she has waited for this day. How she always wanted to find me but didn't know how. How grateful she is that we are finally together.

The decision was made. We called her right away, just in case. We thought we had chosen a good time of day to call. We assumed she was a housewife and would be home alone.

Dancing through the house in her perfectly pressed dress, half-apron around her waist, preparing for her husband's return from his job at the bank, roast in the crockpot, bluebirds fluttering around her.

We didn't want to have an audience. We believed that if she had harbored this as a secret for all these years, her husband might not know. I did not want to expose her past like this.

So I pulled my red flip phone out of my bag and, while we were sitting on the sidewalk outside Zeigler's in this charming South Carolina town, I called her.

She was home.

I was light-headed with nervousness. I was a thirty-three-year-old woman hearing what could be my mother's voice, for the first time.

I wanted to approach her gently. I told her who I was and that I had come to solve a mystery. I was an adopted child, born February 29, 1968, and I was looking for my birth mother. I knew that she was a graduate of the local high school and that she worked for Zeigler's. I had seen her in an ad for the store and wondered if she could help me. "You see," I added, "you look a lot like me." I laughed with the jitters building inside of me.

She denied it vehemently, assuring me that she was sympathetic to my cause, and if she could have helped me she would have. But no, that was not her story. She did work for Zeigler's, and she had forgotten all about that picture, but it was not her. She wasn't even the right age. She was a year younger than my mother.

Brick Wall.

I thanked her and hung up. Carol and I were crestfallen as I recounted the conversation. The more we talked about it, the more we became frustrated that I hadn't asked her the names of other girls she might have known that could have been involved in a story like this one. We should have tried to get more information from her. We shouldn't have given up so easily. We had come too far.

So I called back and apologized for being pushy, but this was something I had always dreamed of. We talked more about her fellow employees. She told me she was only there briefly, for one summer, and she didn't know of any girls that this might have happened to. She was very sweet, and I could tell she wished she could give me some helpful information.

It was then, speaking freely and in a friendly way, that I remembered to ask about Miss Popular. I asked her if she knew this girl in school and where she might be today. She laughed at my theory that if anyone would know the school secrets, it would be her but said she thought it was a great idea. She knew Miss Popular. She gave me her current name and told me she heard she was living in Atlanta, Georgia.

I thanked her, feeling revived. We had another puzzle piece. Where would it fit?

I waited anxiously as the phone rang in Atlanta. As luck would have it, Miss Popular answered.

This was an easier phone call to make. I was not nervous about her being my birth mother, so I appealed to her, woman to woman.

I told her my story, letting her know that I wanted to be very discreet. As far as I knew, my birth mother kept this secret, and I wanted her to know that I was looking for her. I asked Miss Popular if she knew a classmate that this might have happened to, and she said…

"Yes, I know someone that went through this, but let me ask you, why do you think she would want you to find her now? Do you think this is something she would want?"

This was an unexpected question. I stopped in my tracks for a moment but then said, "Yes, I believe she was sad about having to give me up. I think she would want to meet me now and know everything turned out alright."

Miss Popular took this into consideration. She told me that she was not comfortable giving me a name, but she'd make a phone call on my behalf to see if she could help.

We returned home giddy with excitement and proud of all that we were able to accomplish in one day. Why had I waited so long to do this? Days from now, I might know who my birth mother was. This was more than I ever dreamed was possible, and I was elated.

I dropped Carol off late that night, 80's music still ringing in our ears, traces of laughter fading with exhaustion. I thanked her for indulging me all day. She looked at me and said, "Liz, you have never given up. You deserve this. If anyone can do the impossible, it will be you. I know you are going to do it."

ON THE ROAD AGAIN

My father loved to buy older cars. There were many days that Dad would pull up after work with some jalopy or other. My favorite was the 1976 sunshine yellow Volkswagen Beetle. I heard this car drive up before I saw it, its engine drumming down the road like the beating of thousands of hard insects' wings. He was so proud of his latest purchase. I remember him beaming as he walked all around the car, showing it off to my brother and me. *Damn near kicking the tires.* The inside smelled of plastic and leather, and the floor mats had cartoon beetles on them. It was the car I learned to drive a stick-shift in.

Not long after this purchase, Dad announced that he would like to drive up to Conway, South Carolina, and visit some of his Butler relatives. I had never heard of these Butlers before. We didn't really spend time with Dad's family, aside from his sister, Elizabeth, so it was an odd request.

Mom told him immediately that she had no intention of going up there and spending the entire day shuffled from house to house, talking to people she barely knew. I doubt that he even asked my brother, who was well on his way to building the hard, rock island around his solitary lighthouse.

I was twelve, so there were 4,327 other things I would have rather done, but when I looked at Dad, I felt sorry for him. No one wanted to hang out with him, so I said I would go.

We took off on a fall Sunday morning. Daddy felt it was necessary to regale me with an inventory of his family tree so that I would better understand who these Butlers were and how they were related to us. Family names like Virgie, Erline, Coke, Eula Mae, and Zarco peppered the conversation. I wrinkled my nose at the country bumpkin names.

Dad was undeterred, "And then there was Pink; she was Bunnie's sister...."

"Daddy! This is crazy, who names their daughter Pink?"

Dad feigned indignation, "Look here, Elizabeth, I'm ashamed of you! Pink is a perfectly fine name." I looked at him with my arms crossed. "Well, Pink was the eighth child, so maybe they just gave up."

When I was pregnant with my fourth child, I had a list of names a mile long for a third girl (not Pink) and absolutely nothing on the boy list. So, of course, we learned we were having a boy. I recalled this road trip conversation with Daddy as I shared the good news with him about his next grandson. I told him I wasn't sure if there were any good candidates for names from his side of the family, and we laughed at the shared memory.

"Well," Dad mockingly suggested, "I already have a grandson named John, but maybe you could use my middle name, McKager."

"Oh, John,"my mother piped in, left out of the joke, "McKager is the name of a little colored boy living on a farm."

"MOM!" I said, "That is so rude. That is your husband's fine family name you are making fun of. And we don't say colored, Mom, please try to have some political correctness."

Dad laughed, loving to tease my mother.

"Well, anyway," she said.

As it turns out, I did not choose McKager for my newborn son, but if I had had any idea that my Daddy would be dead just fifteen days after my son's birth, you can bet your last dollar I would have.

When we got to Conway and drove up to one of Dad's cousin's houses, I had no idea what to expect. The door opened, and Dad was scooped into a hug by a woman who seemed to be about his age. We were then pulled into the home. Lots of folks were there to say "hi" and catch up.

Everyone came to me and embraced me in big warm hugs. *We were not huggers.* I didn't hug anyone on Mom's side of the family, and this kind of affection was foreign to me. Clearly, my discomfort showed in my body language because one of the ladies grabbed me next and said, "Come on, sweet girl, we are Butlers, and we are huggers." *No, we aren't,* I thought.

I remember looking at Dad and seeing him hug his way around the room and thinking how odd it was that I had never seen my Dad hug anyone before, not even my mother.

I was twelve. I had been raised without a hug.

The ride home was a little quieter than the ride there, with nothing good on the radio apart from the football game, and that had Dad's attention. I wanted to say something about the hugging. I wanted to say that it was really nice to meet his family. I was lost in thought about how to broach this subject when a big fat bug splattered across our windshield and startled us both. We laughed at our own shock.

"Hey, Elizabeth, you know what the bug said right before he hit the car?"

"No."

"It takes guts to do this."

MISS POPULAR

I spent hours on the phone retelling the story of my roadtrip to my friends. I waited anxiously to hear from Miss Popular. It was several long days before she called me back.

I was home alone with the children, and I scrambled for a quiet place to speak with her as I watched them play in the backyard. This could be it. I was so excited to see if she had the final puzzle piece.

"Thank you so much for taking this time to help me, "I started to say as I felt the blood rush faster through my body.

"Well, don't thank me yet, Liz. I don't know if I am going to tell you what you want to hear."

"Oh, I see."

"Now, I called my friend, but I wasn't just going to come out and ask her if she had had a child all those years ago. I just knew that wasn't the right way to approach her if we were going to get anywhere."

"Oh, of course, yes, I can see that," I laughed nervously, waiting for her to get to the point.

"So I called her and I told her that I had gotten a phone call from the nicest young lady. This woman had been adopted, and she had narrowed it down to a woman about our age who might have gone to our school. I told her that I didn't know anything about that, but I would ask around, so I thought to call her and see if she had heard a story like this one."

"Oh, that was good thinking. What did she say?"

"She said she had not, and honestly, Liz, I figured she probably would, but I'm hoping that she has the idea in her head now and maybe she'll come around if she has time, you know, to get over the shock. This couldn't be easy for her."

"No, ma'am, I can't imagine it would." I felt the hit of another brick wall. I watched my daughter scaling the side of her swing set and hoped her little brother didn't get the same idea before I got off the phone.

I didn't want to get off the phone. I wanted Miss Popular's curiosity not to be sated so that she would do something else to help me. She could call her again and try harder. Do something.

"Liz, I did give her your name and your phone number. Please know I told her how kind and lovely you were. I told her that you said you would be very discreet about it."

"Oh, yes, I would," I agreed, hoping to make her help me more, just a tiny bit more.

"I'm still not comfortable sharing her name with you."

Slam.

"I understand."

I did not.

"But she has your name now. That might start something."

"It could, yes, I know." I said, defeated.

It won't.

"Well, thank you for trying, Mrs. *******. I guess we will wait and see."

"We will, darlin'. Why don't you stay in touch with me and let me know if anything happens. I'll be thinking about you; please know I will."

"Of course, you've done all you could. I'll keep on looking. Goodbye, Mrs. *****."

"Wait," she said, "Could I ask you a quick question? Could you tell me what color eyes you have?"

I perked up. She was giving me something. "They are blue, light blue. Does she have blue eyes?"

"Only the most beautiful blue eyes I have ever seen," she said.

Beautiful blue eyes.

A glimmer of hope. *Her hunch was right!*

I began to think every day that this could be it. She might come around. The phone could ring today.

The phone did not ring, and little did I know that I had spoken with my birth mother's high school best friend.

One of two best friends, they called themselves the Three Musketeers. So much for secrets, this Musketeer did not hesitate to call ONE person. My mother now had the advantage. She knew my name. She was prepared.

THE POST AND COURIER

I tried not to let a quiet phone and unanswered questions bother me, but they did. Especially when well-meaning friends who knew my story inquired whether or not there had been any movement in the case.

It was during one of these conversations with a friend, outside my children's preschool, that I was overheard by another mother. She took an interest in my story, and I found myself with eager new ears to delight. However, this time would be different. She was Jennifer Hawes, a feature writer for the local newspaper, and she wanted to do a story about me. Jennifer was also an adopted child, but her story was quite different from mine. She always knew she was adopted and had been sought out by her birth mother at a young age. They had a relationship. It wasn't perfect, but it was good for her.

I eagerly agreed to do this article with her, and we met over coffee so that I could regale her with my entire story. We were there for hours, and it was very exciting to not only tell my story, as I had done a hundred times, but also to have her questions and insights that challenged me emotionally.

The paper asked me to come down for pictures and bring my children. I was so convinced that I looked like my mother that they even did an age progression picture of me to show what I might look like at her age.

The story ran in May 2002.

At the time, I didn't subscribe to the newspaper, so I got up very early that morning and ran to the gas station to pick up a copy. I was just as excited as I had been in the past, getting up at the break of dawn to grab a newspaper and read the reviews of the plays I had been doing for years and years.

This event was much bigger and more exciting. I sat in the car in my sleep t-shirt and shorts with my slippers on and read so that I could have some quiet to think about the story as Jennifer told it, before the children were all over me.

I was really pleased with the article and the story she told. I was glad that people knew how hard it was to do these searches and how I wished I could reach my birth mother. Who knew who might read this article and what changes it could inspire? *Who indeed?*

*It was a Sunday, May 2002. There was a woman in town visiting relatives. It was a long overdue visit, she hadn't been to Charleston in 13 years, so she decided to linger over the Sunday newspaper before driving back to her hometown in SC. She saw the article and read it with interest, because her best friend, from the time they were five years old, had given up a child for adoption and it was a topic that was close to her heart, a secret she had not spoken of in 34 years. Then, she saw the date of my birth and stopped to take a closer look at my face. "Shit," she said and got in her car and drove home fast. She called her best friend the minute she got home, " ******, your daughter is looking for you."

By the time I got home from the gas station, strangers who had seen the article were already calling to share their stories. It was before nine in the morning. The children were up and bouncing around in their playroom, and my husband was leaving for his morning bike ride. He had been against the article all along and was eager to get away from the emotional toll he thought it would have on me. He'd barely even read it. Truthfully, the constant ring of the phone was a welcome distraction from discussing my feelings with him.

The most significant call came from a woman named Heather. She saw my story and had to call me right away. She was born a few months before me in a similar scenario. Her mother also stayed in the Florence Crittenton Home in anticipation of giving her up for adoption. Her family had always been very open about her story *(and she didn't stutter?)*. It was an important one for them because Heather had not been an easy child to place.

She was born with what presented as a heart problem and was turned down by the first family, which was afraid to take a baby that might have health issues. The next family on the list was a pediatrician and his wife, and they accepted Heather despite the worry. As it turned out, she was fine and whatever anomaly they thought would be a problem never materialized.

As she was telling me this tale, it was so hard not to blurt out, "I KNOW THIS STORY." It was my parents who had passed on her. I could have been her. I could have been Heather, the daughter of a pediatrician. So close to having a totally different family, and all these years later to be talking on the phone with her. We took several moments to process this together. What a remarkable coincidence.

When Heather turned eighteen, her family helped her start the search for her birth mother.

Lucky girl. My family still never spoke of it. I never told them anything I had done to search for this woman, my mother. I couldn't imagine they would have any interest in helping me, so I kept it to myself. This article was their first inkling of the desire I still had.

They were very upset about the article. They called me days after it was printed to tell me that I had treated them badly in the article by insinuating that I felt different from the family. I had performed the ultimate act of Southern betrayal; I had aired the dirty laundry. They were getting phone calls of sympathy from the aunts and cousins. I should be ashamed of myself.

Heather completely understood my yearning to know and the difficulties I was facing, but her family had found a private investigator that specializes in reuniting adoptees and their birth families. She offered to share the name of the investigator with me and hoped I would have the same luck.

I was overwhelmed that within hours of this article hitting the streets of Charleston, I had been given the key to unlocking my mystery.

Heather and I said goodbye, and in my singular focus to accomplish future contact with my birth mother, I lost her contact information and never spoke to her again. It is one of my biggest regrets.

I didn't waste any time. First thing on Monday morning, I called the contact that Heather had given me. Yes, the lady was still a private investigator, and she would be happy to help me for $500. It would take some time, but eventually, she guaranteed, I would have all the information I needed.

Guaranteed.

So, again I waited. In the meantime, I sent Miss Popular a copy of the newspaper article so that she could know a bit more about me and perhaps one day try again to speak with ******.

I recalled the agony of being six-, seven-, and eight-years-old waiting for Christmas. It seemed like the days were as long as the whole year. I would do specific things to mark the time. I would set timers to let me know that at least an hour had passed by. I would watch TV. *There's another 30 minutes gone by.* I would go outside and play and run in to see how long I had been active—one hour, maybe less. It was torture. That was nothing compared to the days and weeks that I waited to hear from the investigator.

At least I had my children; they were enough to keep anyone occupied. We spent many hours staying playful and busy to help take my mind off of waiting for the sound of the mail truck. Everything froze for me until my mail lady got closer and closer up the street. It became rather comical to see me dash out the door, waving and getting my mail right in my hands— trying to hide my disappointment as every day brought no news.

As more than a month passed, I began to think that my investigator had gotten the one case that could not be solved; the one seal that could not be cracked. Perhaps my birth parents were even more powerful than the report let on.

My mother was not only from this important, socially upstanding family, but the boy she loved was even more connected. He could be a junior senator from the State of South Carolina, being groomed for bigger and more important things. In her attempts to hold on to him, all secrets were revealed. The shame, the disgrace could never taint his Kennedyesque family name. With a well-placed phone call or a dinner conversation over a single-malt scotch, the records were removed from the Children's Bureau and destroyed.

I was not home, on the day it arrived. Spring had warmed into summer, and we had spent the day at the beach. The beach was always the best place to lose time, and I was grateful for the fun, the sandcastles, and the mud mask for my legs and feet.

For the second time in my life, a manila envelope was sticking out of my mailbox, waiting to give me the information I craved. For the second time in my life, my sweaty, dirty hands grabbed hold of the most important document I had ever seen.

The children had fallen asleep in the car, so I got back inside with them, letting them snooze and sit in the cool of the air-conditioned car while I stared at the envelope.

Here we go. It's all here now. Open it up and see.

LOVE MEANS NEVER HAVING TO SAY YOU'RE SORRY

When I was a little girl, my Daddy never turned on the air conditioning in the summertime. He decided that since we lived on the water, the breezes would keep the house cool. *They did not.* Also, if he turned on the air conditioning, we would just stay inside all summer and not go out to play and be active. *He was right on that one.*

Summers in Mount Pleasant, SC are as hot as all get out.

"As all get out" is Southern for "very." Why use one perfectly good word to describe things when you can use several? Things can be as heavy as all get out or as boring as all get out, etc.

We had large box fans in every window, trying to draw in all the cool air we could find. We downed glasses of iced tea, and we stuck to the furniture.

Nights were sometimes so unbearable that I would sleep on the screened porch, but every once in awhile, a decent night-time storm would blow through. Then we wouldn't have to run around like ants on a bonbon to get all the windows closed because the rain would fall straight down and cool the night air. My bedroom would get so cold I would need a blanket. Those were the best summer nights.

Mom constantly complained to my father about the heat and rightly so. Dad got to go to an air-conditioned office all day, and we were stuck *(literally to the furniture)* at home.

So every August for two weeks or less, Dad turned on the blessed air conditioning, and we had relief. It was magical. The house even smelled better. Cool recycled air.

You could actually sit on the furniture without feeling all scratchy and sweaty. Just as Daddy prophesied, I never went outside. I plopped myself in front of the television and watched movies on our newly installed box that brought cable television into our world.

The summer I was thirteen, I watched *Love Story* with Ryan O'Neal and Ali McGraw. I was hooked. There was about an hour left of the movie when my mother walked by with her basket of laundry and paused for a moment to see what was on.

"Oh, Mom," I said, "you have got to watch this movie. It's so sweet."

"I don't like movies." She really did not. The only movie my mother has ever seen is *Star Wars*, and she hated it.

"No, Mom, really, shhh, sit down."

And much to my surprise, she did. She folded her laundry and got involved in the movie. After a while, she was lying back on the loveseat. Her feet were propped up, and she was hooked, too. She was wearing white ankle socks, and her feet were tapping against each other.

She was content. We were sharing a moment. I kept stealing glances over at her to make sure she was going to stay put. It was like watching a cat—the wrong move and the cat would leap away and go to another room.

By the end, I was crying inconsolably. Mom looked over at me like I was crazy and laughed. Here goes her overly dramatic teenager again. It made her laugh harder.

"What is wrong with you?" she could barely contain herself.

"MOM! Oh my gracious, this is heart breaking. Ali McGraw is dying, and they really love each other, but it's too late and AHHHHHHHH."

Mom stood and picked up her basket, "Oh, I don't know why you made me watch this movie. This was terrible, and you are overly emotional." And she was gone, leaving laughter in her wake.

HELLO, IT'S ME

I was holding the envelope from the investigator in my hands. The car's air conditioning was trying to blow the strands of hair that clung to my forehead, stuck there with sea salt and sand. I hesitated for a second to acknowledge that this was the last moment in my life when I would be in the dark.

Inside the envelope was a letter from my investigator telling me to call her as soon as I had the time to look over everything so that we could discuss the next move.

Page two: Two photographs of an incredibly beautiful girl with pitch-dark hair and piercingly light-blue eyes. The pictures were her junior and senior yearbook portraits, almost certainly xeroxed from the same machine I had used just a few years earlier.

Even in the black-and-white grainy copy, you could tell how light and striking her eyes were. To say that they saw right into you was not an overstatement. I thought she was the most beautiful woman I had ever seen. *She does look like me, I knew it… but so much prettier.* She seemed approachable and kind. I sat and stared at her. Finally, this was her face. This was my mother.

I remembered, all those years ago, seeing this woman in the yearbook. I would have never picked her out as my mother, I thought she was too beautiful. There was no way I looked like that.

I learned her name. Yes, the number of letters matched the blacked out ones I had counted over and over again for years. I said her name out loud. ******. I said my mother's name.

Her birthday was there. Yes, that month would fit what we thought we knew about her from the reports. It was either April or August; we could just see an "A." April. An Aries.

The next thing I saw was a marriage license. She got married about a year-and-a-half after I was born. I looked at the name of this man. I said it out loud. He could be my father. She might have done what she was always planning to do—gone home and resumed their relationship. This was amazing.

She was only married to this man *(my father?)* for about seven years and then divorced him. They didn't have children. Whew. That means I have no blood siblings, if indeed this was the man from my report. In a way I was relieved. IF this man was actually my father and they had gone on with their lives, happily planning a wedding…. Discovering with such joy that they are expecting a baby…. Picking out names together… Shopping for a crib… I would have been so hurt and jealous. Just the thought of it was making my throat close up, so I quickly dismissed it. This is no time for pain, this was delicious discovery. So I switched directions. She just needed to be with him to help her grieve over me, I would think. She needed him to help her forget her past. She needed him like I needed my first ex-husband. A hero to take her away.

She married for a second time about seven years after her divorce. She was still married to this man, and they had two children, a girl and a boy. Perfect nuclear family. I saw no information about the children. I later found out that my investigator was not comfortable giving information about minors. *No problem, they were not my current focus.*

She sent me a photograph of the home my mother was living in, along with her address and phone number.

The house was large and quite stately. She had done well for herself, and her family was very comfortable. That made me happy. She was well. She was, I hoped, very happy. She had children *(well, two of her three).*

I wondered if her husband knew about me. How would she tell him? How could that subject come up?

I spent some time with all this information before I called my investigator. I needed to make sure I could sit quietly and speak to her before the children rallied and needed baths and dinner and Mommy.

We spoke later that evening. She was very pleased with what she had found for me.

"What a lovely woman your mother is, don't you think? You must be so pleased to know she is well," she told me in her deep Georgia drawl.

"Yes, I can't believe it. After all this time. I can see the family resemblances," I told her, looking over all the papers spread out over my dining room table with my mother's photographs dead center. I couldn't stop looking at her.

"Do you really?" she asks, "That is so exciting! I am so happy for you."

"I am curious, though," I added. "I don't see anything at all about my birth father."

"Yes, that part is proving to be rather tricky. We are pretty sure we know who this man is but until we are able to verify it, we cannot give you any information. Surely, you understand. We don't want anyone playing amateur detective and shocking families all over the state, do we?"

Too late for that, I thought with a smile.

"We thought you would want your mother's information right away, so we sent all of that first."

"No, I mean, YES, I am so glad you did. She is my main focus. She is the one that I am most interested in meeting." I held her picture in my hands.

My main focus.

The investigator suggested that I give my mother a call. I could introduce myself and then ask her, "Does the date February 29, 1968 have any meaning for you?"

We could take the call from there. I practiced with the investigator and then I practiced in the mirror for hours. I practiced talking to the grainy black and white high school picture that I had carefully cut off the page in the shape of a heart.

Hello… you don't know me. My name is Liz, and I am calling from Charleston. I was hoping you could help me. Does the date February 29, 1968 hold any special meaning for you? It does? I was born on that day and put up for adoption. I have been searching for my birth mother for a very long time now. It seems all my research, has led me to you. You are? Oh my, I've waited so long to finally meet you. I understand this must be quite a shock, and I want you to take your time, but I'd love to get in my car RIGHT NOW and drive up and hug you so hard!

I might need to take that down a notch. Take two....

I finally mustered up the courage. The children were napping, and all was quiet in the house. I was sitting in my bedroom with her picture, her number, my phone, a salt shaker, a wedge of lime, and a shot of tequila. Just one, I didn't want to be slurry, but I was shaking so much I needed to settle down.

This could all end right now. I would be speaking with my birth mother. I would hear her voice for the first time.

Like my first calls all those years ago, I had waited for a time of day when she should be home alone.

First, the shot. Is it drink, lick, suck, or suck, drink, lick? I never remember.

The phone rang, and she answered right away.

Hello....

"Hello! " *Calm down, breathe, now go!* "My name is Liz, and I am calling from Charleston. I was hoping you had a moment that I could speak with you." I hoped I wasn't speaking too quickly. I tended to do this when I was very nervous.

I tended to speak too quickly even when I wasn't nervous. My father was always telling me to slow down. I could hear his voice in my head at that very moment, "Enunciate properly, Elizabeth!"

I slowed down my speech. It seemed as if the words were being pulled from my mouth like taffy. The tequila burned its way into my body, warming my stomach, easing into my bloodstream.

"Yes," she said.

It's her voice. This is my mother's voice. I closed my eyes to hear it more closely, listening to all the inflections one little word can give.

"Does the date February 29, 1968 hold any special meaning for you?" I held my breath. This was it; this was IT.

"Ah, no, it sure doesn't." she replied.

Wait, what?

"NO?" I started to perspire. I was scrambling, "Oh, well you see Mrs.

**********, that's my birthday. I was born in Charleston and put up for adoption. I was looking for my birth mother and my search has given me your name."

"Well, I'm very sorry, but it's not me." The voice on the other end was clearly confused.

"Oh, well, that's odd. What are the chances that we could have missed this mark?" *Nervous laughter, panic.* I started to fan my shirt on my body to cool down.

"Well, yes, but you did and I'm sorry. Goodbye and good luck." She was clearly done with me.

"Um, yes, well, I, um, thank you."

Click. Hum of the dial tone. I didn't remove the phone from my ear right away. This wasn't right. This wasn't what was supposed to happen. She was supposed to be hesitant, maybe, but eventually happy and excited. This was my big reunion moment and now it was just over. The hum of the dial tone was still in my ear.

She said no.

My face flushed a deep red. I knew this wasn't caused by the tequila. Maybe they had the wrong information. This was horrible. I started to get upset, and I called my investigator to share the news.

She was very gentle with me and assured me that I had done nothing wrong. This was not unexpected. *NOW, you tell me.* It might have just been her first reaction to such a shocking phone call. They suggested I try again, after the news had had time to sink in a bit more.

I agreed and called back. She answered right away, and I apologized for calling back. I just had to be clear. If she wasn't the right woman, then I had to redo my research, so just to be clear this is (I gave her full name).

"No," she said, "that is not my name. My middle name is *****. I get calls for this woman all the time. It's rather annoying."

"So, your birthday is not April 19**?"

"No, it's January, and I am ten years younger than that."

They had the wrong person. I was nervous and upset but so relieved that I laughed.

"I am so sorry for the shock. What a weird day you have just had. HA, HA. Oh my, this is all going to be OK after all." I was almost giddy.

She ended up getting a good chuckle out of it herself. She wished me good luck, and I thanked her for being my trial run! After this call, the real one couldn't be nearly as bad. She was sincerely happy for me. We said goodbye.

The investigator was mortified that she had made such a horrible mistake and called me the next morning with the correct phone number. She assured me that all the other information, including the address, was correct.

Day two.

Today I was more prepared. I was nervous, but I didn't need a drink. I just needed to wait for the right time of day. I was prepared for shock or denial. I was ready to ease her into the fact that I had found her, and I was not going to try to disrupt her life. I was ready to convince her that she needed me just as much as I needed her, and it was all going to be so wonderful.

Bad dress rehearsal, great opening night, isn't that what they say?

"Hello."

I struggled to find my own voice. *This was, finally, the first time I had ever heard my mother's voice.* She had a distinctive Southern accent, much heavier than mine, and I thought instantly that she sounded like an upstate girl.

"Hello, am I speaking to ****** ******* ********?" (I included ALL of her names to make sure this was the right woman. I was not taking any chances this time.)

"Yes you are." *Such a lovely voice.*

Bingo, Brick Wall DOWN. Cue the trumpeting angels. We have arrived.

I just had to get it all out in one breath. I didn't want her to have a chance to hang up or be too busy to talk to me. "My name is Liz, and I am calling from Charleston. If I could just have a minute of your time, I need to ask you, does the date February 29, 1968 have any special significance to you?"

And in the tidy kitchen of her well-appointed home a woman slides down the wall of the room and thinks, Oh, God, this day has finally come.

"Well, no, it doesn't, I'm sorry," she said.

"Oh." I was hoping not to get this response again, but at least this time I was prepared. *You've got this, deep breath.* "Well, that's my birthday. I was born in Charleston and given up for adoption."

"Really?" she asked sympathetically.

She was thinking, she sounds like a Charleston girl.

"Yes, and I have always wanted to find my birth mother and tell her how brave she was and how much I am grateful to her." *Take this slow, Liz. Don't get too excited. Don't say that you really want to be there in time for dinner.*

"That's very nice, but I don't know how I could help you with that," she said.

"Well, it's interesting, Mrs. **********, because I have had the matter looked into, and your name was given to me as my mother."

"I'm not sure how that could happen because it is certainly not me," she is speaking to me like I am a very simple child who does not understand a basic problem.

Brick Wall back up. *Hush up, angel chorus. Quiet now. Give me some more time to think. I cannot let her go.*

I didn't really know what to do next. I was not going to argue with her. She sounded so kind and gentle, and I could hear that she was trying to be very sweet with me. Her voice was really lovely, a genteel Southern woman. I was dead in the water.

"I'm not really sure how that happened either," I said. I was trying hard not to get emotional, and I forced my voice to stay calm, "I guess then, that I am sorry I bothered you. I was just so sure that I was finally heading in the right direction. It's very confusing." I was scrambling. *Just keep talking until you think of something else to say, some magic that will open her up to this.*

"I know it must be. I'm so sorry," she was very nice about it. Very much in control.

Not in control at all, she is sitting on a cold tile floor, the room spinning around her. What is she going to do about this?

"Thank you." I didn't want to hang up. I just couldn't think of anything to say, and there was a moment of silence between us.

"You know," she suddenly broke the silence, "if I were in your shoes I would be doing the same thing you are."

Is this my chance?

"Really? You would?" I used a tone that should have clearly inferred that I was surprised because this was her big moment.

"Yes, I understand," she said.

More silence.

"Well, I'll let you go. I am sorry to have bothered you. Goodbye, Mrs. ********."

I was stunned. It didn't go well at all. She acted as if it wasn't her. She denied me.

How could I fix this? Where could I go from here? This could not be the end. I was thirty-four-years-old. I had waited so long to get this close, to hear her voice, and this was it? This couldn't be the end.

I can get in my car right now, check into a hotel nearby her and wait until the same time tomorrow. I can knock on her door and tell her that it's me. Look at me. Can't you see it? I am your daughter, and I don't know you, but I love you. I have waited so long to meet you. Please just let me come in for one minute. I won't stay long. Please hold me.

Instead, I sat alone and cried.

I was afraid to leave my room at that moment. I did not want to see the looks of sympathy and the "I–told-you-so's" that I would be hearing. I just wanted to change everything that had just happened.

This wasn't what I had always dreamed about. I had gone as far on this journey as I could. This was it. I waited so long to know the truth about my adoption and the few little facts I was given by the state. I waited so long for the actual name and information. I had reached out, and now I was done. I couldn't force myself on her. So this was it. This was where my story ended.

I tried to console myself. After all, she had two young children. I'm not sure how young, but I'm sure she didn't want to have to explain me to them. As a mother, I totally understood this. I didn't like it, but I understood it.

I decided to write her a letter. It was the second very important letter I wrote while tears streamed down my face, and I felt I had come to the end of the road and was lost. The great difference was this letter had the feeling of hope, of a future.

In the letter, I told her that I completely understood what a shock it must have been to hear from me out of the blue. I told her that despite her denial, I was aware that she was, indeed, my birth mother, and I understood her hesitation to speak openly with me. I told her all about my family and myself. I let her know that I was not looking for a big commitment. I would be happy to keep her secret from her family, but if there was any way we could meet, it would mean so much to me.

I included my phone number, my address, and a picture of my children and myself. I sent the letter via certified mail to make sure she got it.

I saved the delivery notice that was sent back to me. She had the most beautiful scrolling cursive handwriting. I liked looking at it.

And I waited.

There was nothing.

YOU HAD THE POWER ALL ALONG, MY DEAR

Years later, and still no word. I spent hours thinking about the journey that had led me to find her. I traveled through the world of What If. Imagining the hundreds of different ways these paths could have led me to her. Would another have been better?

When I was much older, I helped my adoptive mother clean out things from my childhood home. As she aged, and her Parkinson's disease began to claim her freedom and her independence, even in her own home, she began to feel the need to organize her house and get her affairs in order.

It made me sad to see her aging so quickly, but it was shadowed by feelings of annoyance at her extreme attachment to her things. She was seriously expecting me to take time to organize the years of crap she had accumulated. *By the way, she would take great offense at the word "crap." She would say she has very nice things.* I tried to explain to her that Jonathan and I were all grown up. We had our own houses full of crap, *some of my things are actually "crap,"* and what in the world were we supposed to do with her things apart from selling them? *The things I wanted from her were not her fancy antiques and hand woven rugs, they were a piece of costume jewelry she and Daddy had picked up in Florida on their honeymoon, the little collection of ceramic owls that once sat on a shelf in her sewing room, a quilt she had made with her own hands from my baby clothes.* Those were the things precious to me. Well, even this infuriated her. This house was full of her precious possessions.

She insisted that she wanted to make a list of all her furniture and art and choose the child or grandchild who would inherit these things. She called me many times to get going on this project before I had the time to do it. In a way, I felt it was morbid, and I didn't want to help her, but I finally realized that my mother's things were very important to her. They were the constant in her life, the things she could see and touch every day, unlike her children who were fleeting visitors at best. She needed to believe that they would be handled properly after she was gone.

We spent an entire day going from room to room. She told me what each piece meant, either where it came from or who bought it for her. We carefully and fairly decided who would need it and love it. She was very satisfied when we were done, but I could see that the day had taken its toll on her.

"OK, Mom, you really look exhausted. I'm going to take this home and type it all up and get it back to you; one copy for each of us and one for the attorney."

"No, Elizabeth, we haven't done the china and the things in the hutch in the dining room." She had already pulled herself out of her chair with the help of her three-pronged cane with tennis balls on the bottom. She didn't quite have the strength to make it, so I walked over and held her around the waist to steady her.

"You got this?" I asked before I let go.

"Yeah." She headed in the direction she wanted to go. No one was telling Katherine Butler what she could and could not do.

Once we reached the dining room, I pulled out a chair for her, and she plopped down with all her weight. Tired.

"Mom, don't you want to go lie down?" I pleaded.

"I'm here. I'm going to do it."

The hutch was loaded to the brim, like every other nook and cranny of the house. A lifetime collection of things. I saw so many pieces from my childhood that hadn't seen the light of day in ages.

"Oh, look, Mom, these are the candle holders for the advent wreath!" I showed them to her excitedly, "I used to love it when these came out. It was the only time you allowed candles to be lit in the house. Do you remember?" I held them close as memories came flooding back of the house decorated at Christmas and all the excitement that came with it. "I still love the smell of a blown-out match. It will forever remind me of Christmas."

"Well, then, you take them if you want them. Take them now. I won't be using them again."

"You're sure?"

"It's fine, Elizabeth," she sighed.

We moved more things around—some white serving pieces for my daughters, some sterling silver for my brother. His wife had chosen the same silver pattern, so it was good to keep them together. *Clever girl.*

"Now, what in the world is this?" I removed an old ceramic bootie. It was a vase that would have held a small flower arrangement. It was pink and white and quite old.

"Well, that was delivered when we got you. *(This is how she will always refer to my adoption. When we got you.)* Lord if I remember who sent it. It used to be in your nursery."

So not THAT old.

"It's all cracked and glued back together," I noted.

"I'm sure you did that at some point. You were always jumping around. Daddy glued it back together."

She always referred to her husband as Daddy. I never heard her call him John until we were much older. The thing that has always stuck in my craw was that when she talked about my brother, she always, and without fail, called my father "His Daddy." Always. Every time. Even when she was talking to me about them, she would say something like, "Jonathan is out with His Daddy." She didn't do it on purpose, and if I called her out on it, she would think I was being overly sensitive. But I always thought "my Daddy, too."

"I don't know why it's in there," she said. "You can just throw it away."

"No." I said holding it, staring at it. "I think I'll keep it."

"That old thing?" she laughed.

"Yeah, I think I love it. It's a lot like me, Mom. It came into this house; it got a little broken up; but it's OK now. Just like me, don't you think?" Tears began to sting the backs of my eyes, but I smiled.

"Well, anyway." she shrugged.

I quickly turned back to my work.

"Now then, take your book, too," she said pointing with her cane to a white box in the back of the hutch. On the top it said, "All About You."

Inside was a baby book of the same name, still in the plastic jacket cover. It was my baby book.

"Yeah, OK," I laughed, "I saw this as a child. I was so excited, and I opened it up and there was nothing in it."

It was always a bone of contention for me that there were seemingly hundreds upon thousands of pictures of my brother and ten of me *(my exaggeration)*. And of those ten, Jonathan was in eight. His baby book was meticulously filled out in Mom's distinctive handwriting, and mine was all but empty.

"What!" she exclaimed. She didn't remember.

I opened it and flipped the first few pages. "Nothing, nada. Just a list of presents I got and the church program from my baptism. Oh, look, there is a picture in here! Oh, it's of Jonathan."

"Oh, Elizabeth, you do go on so." We both laughed. *I loved that I could finally laugh at things like that.*

"Well then, take it anyway." She dismissed the conversation with a wave of her shaky hand. "What am I going to do with it now? I can't write in it. I can't hold a pencil well anymore, and besides, I can't remember what I wore yesterday."

"Great, Mom, that just warms the heart." I returned the book to its box, and I tossed it on the table. It spun a bit so that I could see the side of the box. I had never seen this before. I had looked at the inside, not the outside. The box flap read, "All About You: An Adopted Child's Memory Book."

I froze.

The answer had been staring at me from the hutch all along. I was flabbergasted. How did I not see this? THAT was the smoking gun that I had torn the house apart looking for as a teenager, cracking a family secret! I had it all along, just like Dorothy's ruby red slippers. I could have skipped the entire yellow brick road. All the turmoil, all the flying monkeys.

Later, after the inventory was done, I left. Mom insisted on walking me to the door to make sure it locked behind me, but she had to stop in the foyer and sit down for a minute.

"Just watch me, Mom. I'm turning the handle. When the door closes, it will be locked behind me. I'll even test it."

"Fine, Elizabeth, go on." She was breathing a little heavily, and it gave me pause to look at her, so old and defeated.

"We got a lot done today, you know, Mom. It's all taken care of."

She nodded, put her shaky hands in her lap, and sighed. With the expulsion of air, her shoulders sagged, and she just kept nodding.

I backed out the door with that image in my mind. I carried my candlesticks and my book and my little broken shoe to my car.

Once inside the car, I tried to put the key in the ignition, but I was crying too hard to see it. I sat there for quite some time.

GUY INCOGNITO

Years passed from the day of that fated phone call to my birth mother.

I thought of my birth mother often, thoughts followed immediately by the memory of rejection. The sting of that feeling crept up whenever I felt insecure. I continued to tell my story to people who wanted to hear it. Only now it had a dramatic ending. *And she didn't want to meet me, so there you have it. And, yes, it's very hard to take, but what can I do?*

I often thought about going back to the upstate to spy on her.

I could park in the neighborhood by her house, wait for her to leave, and follow her. I could bump into her in the same grocery store walking down the same aisle. Our carts would "accidentally" bump into one another. "Oh, gracious, I'm so sorry," I'd say. "How clumsy of me! Do you know where they stock the lemon curd in this store?" (Anything to keep her talking so that I could get a good look at her. All I had was this grainy high school yearbook picture. I wanted to know what she looked like NOW). "Oh, the lemon curd, that's over here. I'll take you that way."

OR

I could drive up there, poke a roofing nail into my tire, and then drive through her neighborhood until the tire was good and flat. I'd end up in front of her house and knock on the door, asking to have her call a tow truck for me. Of course, she would invite me in. (I'm very charming.) We would have to sit and wait, and maybe she would make me some tea. We would have a lovely chat.

Fortunately, I did none of those things, but I spent lots of time talking about the trip. I had friends ready and willing to go with me. There had to be a way to figure out what she looked like now. It was the last thing I could obsess about. I had found her. I had spoken with her. Now for a picture, please.

Let's be very clear. If I heard that someone was looking for me and ONLY had my high school yearbook picture to know what I looked like,

I would move hell and high water to get to them and remove that image from their minds forever.

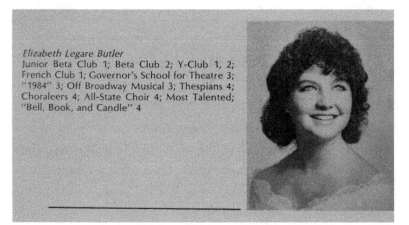

Elizabeth Legare Butler
Junior Beta Club 1; Beta Club 2; Y-Club 1, 2; French Club 1; Governor's School for Theatre 3; "1984" 3; Off Broadway Musical 3; Thespians 4; Choraleers 4; All-State Choir 4; Most Talented; "Bell, Book, and Candle" 4

My high school senior portrait. Where was the Ambush Makeover Team when I needed them? Is that a MULLET?

I hired a private investigator. He was going to send me pictures. He charged a lot of money that I did not have to spend frivolously, but I knew it would be worth it.

I imagined pictures of her getting into her car, looking over her shoulder, large Jackie-O sunglasses on her face. Another photo of the outside of her lovely home; she is waving to a neighbor, head tossed back in laughter. Another outside her church, shaking the hand of the old minister, smiling and holding the hand of a child, maybe a girl that looks just like me, too.

He called back with bad news. The fancy neighborhood she lived in didn't really allow for reconnaissance. The driveways were behind the houses, and you drove down a narrow road to gain access to them. This was not conducive to sitting idly in a car. He would surely be noticed. He tried and failed and that was all he could do for me, unless I wanted to pay him more. I did not have more money to give him. Once again, I got so close.

DO ME A FAVOR

Over the years, I never talked to Mom and Dad about looking for my birth mother. It was an understandably sore subject that was pushed under the rug along with everything else.

They still fumed about the newspaper story. They thought I had portrayed them unfairly; they were just doing their best. I understood how they felt, now that I was watching my own children spin around me with all the unexpected moods and tantrums that occupy even the youngest minds. I told them how easy it was for me to look back on the past and make judgments. All children do it, even before they are old enough to understand what their parents go through loving and raising a child. You make mistakes and you never hear the end of it, but you keep going. What we missed out on was true communication. We had it in the beginning, as soon as we learned language.

"Ba Ba!!" my two year old son would demanded reaching for the sippy cup just out of arms reach, his chubby face turning pink with exertion.

"It's not a Ba Ba, Aidan. Use your words. I can't help you if you don't use your words." I say in that stupid overly calm "mother" voice I hear coming out of my face.

If only we would continue to "use our words" all the time as we grow. Speak your truth. Talk. Don't keep it inside. Don't cover pain with flowery words. Don't BA BA over the feelings.

I reminded them that I would not be content to live my whole life never knowing anything about the woman who had given birth to me, and I couldn't understand how they didn't have sympathy for that.

"That is the past," my mother said. It entered the list of things you didn't talk about, like who you voted for in the last election; how much money you make; the fact that anyone in her family history might have owned another human being; and whether or not you dyed your hair.

I wanted them to see for themselves that my birth mother had been an upstanding young woman who made a mistake. I thought she deserved their respect. I was proud of her. I loved that I looked like her and that she looked like my children. I wanted my parents to see that and be happy for me and see the good that had come out of that article.

So it was rather begrudgingly that I shared with them the information that I had to date. I carefully compiled my Non-Identifying Information and the reports I had gotten from my first investigator to share with them.

I would never tell them about the investigator. I had already heard enough from my soon to be EX- second husband about the unscrupulous people just waiting to take advantage of me and my wallet.

I drove over to our family home in Mount Pleasant to sit in the same den I sat in, with such shame, so many years ago and talked about my adoption. We took our exact positions on newer sofas.

My father was particularly taken with her picture. He thought she looked just like my daughter and my mother agreed. I thought it was interesting that they made it all about my daughter and not me. It gave them that wall between my birth mother and themselves, they would not let it touch them directly...or me.

"Well, what are you going to do now?" My father asked.

"Oh, well, I called her last week."

They both looked at me with interest.

"She said it wasn't her; she denied it."

Silence from them both. Eyes cast back down on the picture.

"My investigator says to give it time. She might come around."

"Don't get your hopes up, Elizabeth," my mother said, rising and heading off to the kitchen to finish making dinner. "She may never be ready."

Dad handed me back the pictures, and I packed everything back up in the envelope.

"So," he cleared his throat, "how much did all this cost you?"

"Not as much as you'd think. The investigator could have really taken me to the cleaners, and I would have paid, but it was only $500."

He stood up, "Wait right here before you go."

I stood and waited by the door. He returned, rather sheepishly, with a check written out to me for $500.

"I want to cover the cost of this for you. I know that's a lot of money."

"It's OK, Dad, I got this," I said.

"No, now, I should be helping you with this. I know how much it means to you."

We stood there, looking at each other. I knew at that moment that this was Dad trying to tell me he was sorry, and giving me this check was his way of helping and showing support. There were still no "I love yous," but this, for him, was the next best thing.

"Do me a favor," he said, handing the check to me, "if you ever get to meet her, I want to get a chance to meet her, too."

I didn't know what to say, so I hugged him. *We are Butlers and we are huggers.*

He didn't have to buy his way in. I would have taken him anyway.

SOCIAL MEDIA

Facebook, the social media giant that would be the beginning and end of so many relationships.

As soon as I joined in 2008, I made a point of looking for my birth mother. She was not on Facebook, but I wondered if her children were.

It had been seven years since that disappointing phone call. So much had changed. So many people were all over the Internet, including myself.

The whispers got louder. "You know," she suddenly broke the silence of that long-ago phone call, "if I were in your shoes, I would be doing the same thing you are."

I wondered.

I did not know her children's names. Their names and the name of my birth father were never revealed to me.

I was stuck again. I randomly checked to see if she had joined Facebook, but there was always nothing.

Years later, another website took the internet by storm: Ancestry.com.

I searched Ancestry.com for my birth mother and found her on a census record as a child. There she was, with her mother and father, my birth grandparents. Once I knew the names of her parents, it was easy to find them. I discovered that they had passed away after living long lives. *Wait, they died. That meant there was an obituary, and obituaries have all kinds of family names in them and THAT is public record.*

The deceased is survived by his daughter ********* and her children ******** and ***.

Bingo. The Brick Wall cracks.

I found my sister on Facebook right away. One of her Facebook friends had the same name as the brother I had found in the obituary, so I knew I had the right kids. Not kids, though, all grown up.

My sister's profile picture? The place you represent to the Facebook public what you look like? A Boykin Spaniel?

Oh, I think, that might not be good. In my Facebook experience, people usually put their dogs or their kids as profile pictures if they don't like the way they look. Maybe she's shy and insecure.

My brother's profile picture? He was holding a couple of beers and wearing large sunglasses. College kid.

I had found them, but I still could not see what they looked like. Would this frustration ever end? Could I at least see if we had any sibling resemblances?

My brother's Facebook activity was very limited, so I focused on my sister. *My sister!* All of her privacy settings were on, so I was blocked from seeing her personal information and any of her pictures, except her profile picture. There was no hope of snooping.

I checked back every once in awhile *(OK, almost daily and no, that is not stalking, that is just checking in)*, and the profile picture finally changed. It was a person in a Cinderella character outfit with a baby on her lap. *Did she have children? Were they at Disney World?*

I needed to work harder to crack the case. I finally thought, why not just google her and see if she has done anything news worthy? *Maybe she has a blog teaching people how to train dogs and plan family vacations to Disney World.*

And there she was and she was an actress. She did theatre, just like me. And she was good; she had leading roles. She looked like me. My friends saw it even more than I did. A sister. I have a sister. I could look at her.

It turned out she was not visiting Cinderella, she WAS Cinderella in that picture. I saw it clearly now. She was doing an event. She looked to be in her mid-twenties.

I decided to send her a friend request. She had hundreds of friends; what's one more?

She did not take the bait. My *sister* is a careful girl. OK, that's good. Not good for me, though.

I tried again and attached a note. Some total BS about moving to her town and looking to meet other theatre folks.

She didn't fall for that one either. I'm worried now that she is thinking I am some total nut job.

Then Mother's Day rolled around. Everyone on Facebook was posting images of themselves with their mothers. It was so nice to see them all and then it hit me. Wait, themselves with their MOTHERS! I opened my sister's page, and there they were: mother and daughter, their arms around each other in a casual embrace, wearing large black sunglasses. *SERIOUSLY!* What is with these people? Do they sell sunglasses? Why can't they remove them for the camera?

I decided it was time. I needed to write another letter to my birth mother to see if now, after all this time, she would agree to meet me. Her kids were grown; it would be so much easier. I started to compose the letter. Deleting it; rewriting it. I tossed and turned on sleepless nights and wondered how I should approach her yet again.

Then there was the January 2011 Oprah Winfrey Show.

Oprah had a shocker for the viewers that day. She had a long-lost sister.

I watched this episode, fascinated. I don't think I moved for the entire hour. This woman had known Oprah was her sister for a long time. She had reached out but never really pressed the issue. She handled it very well, Oprah's sister. You could see in the interview that she was clearly not after Oprah for her wealth and fame. She was only looking for that family connection, filling that hole that most all adopted children share. She was very interested in meeting Oprah's mother—her mother, too.

Oprah's mother was not open to the idea, and viewers saw a very tender moment when Oprah faced the camera and assured her mother that what she did was brave and noble and the best she could have done for this daughter of hers. There was no need to feel shame anymore. Let the shame go.

It was my big moment of realization, my *Ah ha* moment. Shame. What a powerful emotion my birth mother might have felt. It might even be tinged with guilt. *I gave away a baby.*

I could see clearly now that my mother was never going be able to break down this wall and let me into her life. It was all too shameful. How could she explain it to her children? To her husband? It was never going to work for me. No letter, no phone call, no accidental meeting in the grocery store would ever work.

If I was going to have any chance of meeting her and being any part of her life, I had to go through my sister.

I thought and thought about it. I composed this letter a hundred times until I was finally brave enough to send it.

Facebook message sent June 11, 2011:

I sent a friend request to you a month or so ago. I was hoping we could get to know each other on Facebook, as superficial as that could be, for a bit before I sent you this message.

I hope this isn't too shocking for you to hear, and I do hope this is not the first you have heard of this, but I fear it probably is, and for that I am sorry. However, I wanted to reach out to you and have wanted to for quite some time.

So, here we go. On February 29, 1968 ****** ***** ******* gave birth to a girl she put up for adoption. That was me. I was adopted by Dr. and Mrs. John Butler of Mount Pleasant, SC and grew up in a privileged household. I was not aware I was adopted until I was 15. It came to me as the shock that perhaps this is coming to you. My hope is that with you being older and wiser than a 15-year-old girl, you will be able to process what I am telling you in a way that won't damage the relationship you have at home. What ****** did was hard for her, I'm sure. She was brave. She gave me a wonderful life without the shame my life with her would have caused her family back in the 1960s. I have nothing but respect for her.

Ten years ago, I searched for her, once I had the first two of my four children. Finally having someone in my life that I could look at and see ME made me yearn to meet this woman more than ever. And believe me, the desire had burned deeply in me for all those years. I only have one picture of her, a Xerox copy from her yearbook. I have never seen another.

I hired an agency that got my original birth certificate, and I contacted your mother. She was not open to meeting me, but I have to say she was very compassionate with me on the phone. She took the (expected) route of denying it. I did not push it. I wrote her a letter shortly after telling her I would not pursue her again, that I understood she had young children and I did not want to rock her world. Who knows, her own husband may not know and I imagine that would be scary for her.

So I waited all these years to try and find you. I wanted you to be old enough to have compassion for your mother's secret and privacy. I wanted you to be able to meet me, if you would like, and "vet" me and see if your mother ever wanted to meet me. Of course, we could merely be FB friends for a while so you could look into me and my life to assure yourself that I am not a freak. I am not needy emotionally, I am not poor. I am looking for a connection. Not a sister. Maybe one day, we would get there, but I am not one to push myself on anyone. This is your choice. It's been ten years since I made an attempt to meet your mother. I hope this alone proves to you that I was not a stalker or a weirdo. If you did friend me, rest assured I WILL NOT make mention of this in a public forum. I will NOT pressure you to meet me.

The interesting thing about finding you, well there are many, but we are both theatre girls. My adopted family was NOT, in ANY way, but that part of me could not be denied, and I have been an active theatre performer since I was 16. You can google me. You will see that I am an accomplished wedding and portrait photographer, a wife and mother of four. A theatre regular. And a good friend.

Please take your time. I apologize for the shock. But if I were you, I would have wanted to know. And not to sound like a total dork, but when Oprah had her sister on the show, I had my AH HA moment about you.

I sent that message at 2:00 in the afternoon. I was leaving shortly after that to go to work. I was photographing a wedding on an island that did not have proper cell towers, and I knew I would be completely unable to obsessively check my messages. I could allow time to pass and maybe my sister would see it.

I was thinking about it constantly, though. I could not stop that train. All day long, I second-guessed my move. What if I had upset her? What if she was some horrible spoiled brat who wanted nothing to do with me? What if she thought I was lying or scamming her and never even responded?

I prayed. I did that a lot, and that day was as good a time as any to ask the universe to help me, to assure me that I had done the right thing. So I asked for a sign. I knew it had to be unique. I knew it had to be something out of place.

The first word to pop into my head was "feather." Well, that's not unusual. I was on an island, and there were birds everywhere. Then I had the thought, *a feather you would never see on a beach.*

Fine.

The wedding went very well. The pictures were turning out beautifully; the sunset was amazing; and we wrapped up the portrait session on the beach and started to head to the reception. I was laughing and joking with the couple when I bent down to get my shoes, and right there, a few feet away, I saw a feather. A peacock feather. You didn't ever see that on the beach. I had my sign, and my spirits were immediately lifted. I was full of hope.

I returned home to find a message waiting for me from my sister— sent the same day, just five hours after mine.

My email dinged on her phone while she was backstage preparing for a show in her hometown theatre. She was wearing a lobster costume and waiting for the curtain to rise on a matinee production of a children's musical. Later, even she laughed about this strange moment of having to conduct herself as the most believable lobster while her brain was spinning with information. She had to anxiously wait for the show to end before trying to contact her (our) mother to find out if this was true. After the show my sister high tailed it over to her (our) mother's house and pulled her aside from the rest of the family, gathering for their typical Saturday meal together.

My sister mentioned that they sat outside on a bench in the backyard, the sun was starting to slowly set casting long shadows on the ground that seemed to be leaning into them listening to their whispers. She wasn't quite sure where to begin so she blurted it all out at once, "this email arrived and I don't understand what's going on, could this even be true? Who is this woman?"

My mother sat in stunned silence, eyes barely able to focus on her daughter's face. She looked at my sister and began to cry as the confession of her most deeply held secret poured from her heart. She was a young unmarried woman when this happened and she was scared and didn't know what to do. Only her best girlfriend and her parents knew. And until this day, with the loss of her parents and the trust in her lifelong friend, the secret had been hers to keep.

How many times in how many years had she found herself moving throughout her day and thoughts of me would creep in, did she suddenly stop what she was doing, did her eyes soften as her mind drifted to another time, another place, did she linger in that fog of memory until the sounds of her children clamouring into the room returned her to the tasks at hand. …

Based on our mother's response my sister gently informed me that she was not ready to meet me yet. She needed time to get over the shock and adjust. Unbeknownst to me there were other family issues going on simultaneously, and the combination set her into a tail spin.. Family, I think, one day maybe we will be a family. I find myself split between feeling excited and devastated all at once. *But I am here! I am ready now!*

My newly found sister and I made a plan to speak on the phone. She said she had a million questions for me. And, I had a million and one for her.

We made a date to talk the very next night. It was not lost on me that it was the night of the Tony Awards, and the "theatre" sisters would be talking for the first time.

Brick Wall begins to CRUMBLE.

We were on the phone that night for an hour-and-a-half. There was so much to say and ask. I decided from the beginning that I would just let her do all the talking. There was no need for me to get too excited. I would remain calm.

It really wasn't necessary because we had a great talk. It flowed easily, getting to know each other and letting her tell me about her family. She had questions for me about my life, curious if we had ever done any of the same plays. Our conversation was filled with more than just pleasantries. It was sincere.

I asked a lot of questions about our mother. I mainly wondered what kind of mother she was. How did she feel about her theatrical daughter? Was she supportive?

Turns out she is a very supportive theatre mom. She did not limit herself to merely being a spectator; she volunteered backstage. They even dragged our poor brother around, and he often found himself in the background. *Townsperson number one.*

However, now was indeed a hard time for them. Her father was a recent cancer survivor and, afterwards, his personality unexpectedly changed. This quiet, kind man was suddenly argumentative and making rash decisions in business and life. He'd left my mother and all but ignored his children. It was heart-breaking to hear that all this was happening.

She was right. I could not have chosen a worse time to try to meet my mother; yet I could not have chosen a better time. They were a broken family, and they might have never needed a ME in their lives, but they did now.

My sister suffered a great loss with the absence of her father, and without either of us really knowing it at that moment, I had arrived at just the right time to fill that void.

My sister ended up being my savior and I hers. I gave her something to think about that was hopeful, not hopeless. I was a gain in the midst of her loss. We were the perfect balm for each other.

We ended our first conversation on a high note. I asked her for a favor before we hung up. I told her that I had never seen more than a high school picture of my mother and asked her to send me one. I didn't want her to think she wasn't equally important to me, so I asked for one with the two of them together. She agreed, and I hung up, elated. I was going to finally see a proper photograph of my mother. I would see my family, maybe even my new brother.

JONATHAN

We are 7 and 11 years old, it is an early Saturday morning and we are racing through the house. We are pushing and shoving without mercy because the stakes are high. First one to the TV gets control of what we are watching. I want to watch Scooby Doo but he prefers the Super Friends. I hate the Super Friends, I think they are boring. We are nearing the end of the hall getting closer to the family room when Jonathan makes a bold and calculated move, he shoves me into the entrance to the formal living room as we pass by on a curve and I lose my balance and slide dangerously close to the antique coffee table with the precious ceramic piece that has been in my mother's family for generations. By the time I recover, he is ensconced on the sofa, the TV is on and Mikey is about to love that bowl of LIFE cereal.

"That's not fair!" I insist, out of breath and steaming mad.

"Get out of the way, I can't see the TV." Jonathan replies throwing a pillow at my head.

"I was ahead and you played dirty, you cheated, so I win."

"You can't cheat when there are no set rules."

"Yes you can."

"Don't talk if you don't know, Liz." He retorts, second pillow whizzes past my little afro.

Oh, that phrase. *Don't talk if you don't know.* If I heard it one time, I heard it a million. It made me so mad every time, I could have pulled out my hair if it was long enough to grab hold of. It caused me to stomp my feet and fight back tears of frustration. *Don't talk if you don't know, Don't talk if you don't know.*

When I told Jonathan I was writing this book he immediately said, "I'm thinking of writing one too, I'm going to call it 'Don't Talk if You

Don't Know'." We both burst into gales of laughter but there was still a small part of me that felt rage start to bubble up in my gut wanting to ball my fist up and punch him in the face... *old habits.*

I know I was an annoying little sister, but I wanted to be a part of his world and I wanted secret access to the Lighthouse. There were many times I was let in and it was magical.

My favorite memory was Christmas Eve when I was ten. Jonathan made a radio out of a kit *(of course he did)* and it had a microphone that you could use to hear yourself talk or sing. Well, this particular night, Jonathan snuck into my room and quietly led me back into his domain. He had opened the attic access door in his room. It was a tiny door, only there to provide service to the chimney. Jonathan had opened the chimney shoot door and fed the microphone with it's cord down the length of the chimney to spy on Mom and Dad, busy preparing the room for Christmas morning. I remember being so nervous and afraid we would get caught. I was trying so hard to suppress the nervous giggles that threatened to bubble up out of my throat and exploded into the tiny space echoing all throughout the chimney and get us busted. I was wiggling around in my excitement and finally had to fly back into my room and hide under the covers I was so wracked with guilt and nervous energy.

The older he got, the more he naturally pulled away. The more I would irritate him and cause him to snap at me.

Looking back on all our childhood arguments and all the insults that were thrown back and forth, he sure had a doozy he could have whipped out at any time. *(Of course he never did.)*

"Oh, yeah, well, you're not even really my sister, you are ADOPTED."

"I am not, take that back..."

"Don't believe me? Fine, but, you are. Your real family didn't even want you."

I wonder if he ever thought about it, or if he did but he had to pack it up tight and move on to the next little sister bashing idea he could come up with. Maybe that was what all the doors slammed in my face meant... this fight is over, don't make me hurt you. *Don't talk if you don't know.*

Despite my brother doing his best to keep a cool distance between his emotions and our family, I still felt like he let me in more than anyone. I learned to take the time he doled out to me and not pressure him for too much more. I got his sense of humor and I grew to love and admire him so much. The words that had once stung me *"So, are you JONATHAN Butler's little sister?"* I now wear proudly like a beauty pageant banner. Look at me, I am Jonathan's sister.

Liz Butler Duren

SISTER

Despite our fantastic phone call, my sister did not send me a picture.

We continued to keep in touch on Facebook. She still did not accept my request to be her Facebook friend. She was moving slowly and taking her time. This was killing me. I had waited so long, and now I was as close as I would ever be, but information was being handed out in very small doses.

We spent more time emailing and getting to know one another.

The process was a delicate dance, a careful exchange of *hello's* and *thinking about you's* and *how are things?* She led and I followed, clinging tightly and trying to anticipate the footing and sways in our *pas de deux.*

She dips me: '*I spoke to Mom today and told her all about your theatre success and she was so excited about everything you have done.*' I melt gracefully in her capable hands: '*that's amazing, I can't wait to see a picture of her!*' She sets me down slowly, turns and takes off and just as suddenly leaves the floor in a grand jete leaping away: '*TTYL, gotta run, thank you for being so patient, I am grateful for the grace you have shown our family.*' I curtsey: '*of course, take your time.*' She chaines around me: '*I had dinner with Mom and I brought my ipad to show her pictures of you. She was really happy to see them and how pretty you are.*'

I freeze in my steps halting our dance. '*She saw me. What did she think? What did she say?*'

'*She said you look like her mother, you definitely got the ******* family genes, especially the eyes.*'

'*But, she didn't seemed surprised to see you,*' hinting that our Mother had done some sleuthing of her own and looked me up on the internet.

I look like a *******. That was the most wonderful thing anyone had ever told me.

So, she HAD looked for me.

Of course, she had my name from the calls and the letter.

Over the years, I wondered if she was thinking about me. *She was.* When I had roles in plays and reviews published about them in the paper, I wondered if she would ever get to see my successes. *She did.*

This was remarkable news to me.

"You know," she suddenly breaks the silence, *"if I were in your shoes, I would be doing the same thing you are."*

My sister and I continued our correspondence over the following weeks. A lovely friendship was forming and a comfortable banter developing. Still, no picture of my mother. She was holding back, keeping me at arm's length and doling out information when she felt ready, keeping herself safe…. keeping her mother safe. It wasn't OK, but it was something, and I was clinging to it with all my hopes. I jumped whenever I saw a new message come from her, and I would share it with my husband, gushing about my sister.

I was in rehearsal for a play, a lighthearted comedic romp that we were staging for a summer release. My best friend Keely was directing. Keely and I had met just after I had found and lost my birth mother.

Keely, a California girl who left swimming pools and movie stars behind to live in the land of Scarlett O'Hara, was lively and smart, and my last name was BUTLER! (Frankly, my dear, we were meant to be together.)

Her dream: open a theatre and produce thoughtfully written productions with the most gifted local actors (I added that part). She was a fast-talking go-getter and her dream came to fruition. I was lucky enough to be cast by her and our friendship blossomed instantly.

She was fascinated by my adoption story and her heart was broken over its tragic abeyance and my inability to find the answers I sought. We would sit together long after rehearsals ended in a darkened theatre discussing the nuances of the story, psychoanalyzing the characters involved, and plotting the next steps that would bring me closer to a reunion.

So, it was only fitting that the first time I ever saw an actual photo of my mother I was with her.

Rehearsals were in full swing and during my time off stage I sat in the back of the theatre watching my friends perform. I tilted back the metal chair I was sitting in, balancing precariously on the table behind me. My iPhone vibrated in my pocket. It was a message from Facebook.

My one-year-old friend request to my sister had been accepted.

The shock and surprise propelled me from my chair, which tumbled over loudly onto the floor. Rehearsal abruptly stopped as all eyes turned to stare in my direction.

"Are you alright?" Keely asked

"It's my sister's Facebook!" I shrieked, my voice an octave so high in range that it might have awoken a few neighborhood dogs, "I'm in!!"

"What?" Keely leapt from her seat and was suddenly by my side peering over my shoulder.

"Look at all of these pictures!" I said. "My mother must be in some of them!"

My confused cast members watched this exchange not knowing what to do next without direction or motivation.

"Start looking Liz, I'm so excited," Keely encouraged me before turning back to the stage.

"Sorry folks, big moment here," she explained. "Liz has the most interesting adoption story…." She regaled the cast with my story as I began scrolling through hundreds of pictures deemed Facebook worthy.

My beautiful sister in high school. Dances. Sleepovers. Beach trips.

My beautiful sister in college. Roommates. Boyfriends. Football games.

Where is her mother?

My beautiful sister graduates. Parties. Debutante Balls. Weddings.

And then I find her.

My mother.

She was standing beside my sister at a party or some kind of special event. My mother had dark brown shoulder-length hair with just a smattering of gray peeking through. Her bright blue eyes were full of life and laughter. She seemed very happy to be standing there next to her daughter.

I was seeing my mother for the first time in full color as a grown woman, not just some Xerox copy of a teenage girl.

I was forty-three years old.

I dashed to Keely's side and whispered, "There. That's her."

"Liz," she stared at the picture and at me and laughed out loud, adding "this is so clearly your mother. Look at her! The resemblance is overwhelming. I don't look this much like either of my parents!"

"I know." I was staring at the photo, captivated. Emotions were everywhere: I can't believe it's her...why doesn't she want me...she's so pretty...I'm so mad that she won't meet me…

The other actors wandered over, each of them struck by the resemblance I shared with this virtual stranger. Their expressions of delight and surprise bursted around me like fireworks and all I could do was *ooohhh* and *ahhhhhh* with them.

I wanted so badly to move this along to get a chance to meet her, but I knew I had to take my time with this family. They were all so broken right now. I could only hope that I would find my way in.

I enjoyed getting to know my sister. We were regular pen pals now, and we shared in the simple events that happened in each other's lives. She mentioned she was cast in a musical that was opening soon in her town's little theatre and how grateful she was for the experience. It would give her something to do and focus on as she dealt with all her family drama.

I decided to go see this show. I didn't tell anyone I was going, especially not her. I was planning to just sit in the dark and see the play and leave. I was so anxious to watch her. I was interested in how she did and wanted to hear her sing.

My current *(and last, I swear!)* and most supportive husband, Rob, was excited to go with me, and we chose a Sunday matinee. It was likely that my mother would not be there. She would have gone to see opening night or at least an evening performance. So off we went.

We arrived early, so we skulked about in a restaurant next door and indulged in a Bloody Mary *or two*. I needed this; my nerves were off the charts. What if my mother was there? I didn't know how I would handle that. This wasn't really the time or place.

The performance we went to was a children's musical. We ended up being the only adults there without children. We got a good laugh out of that, which helped calm me down as I searched the crowd. I saw no sign of anyone who looked like my mother, so I relaxed and watched and waited to see my sister for the first time.

Lights up and there she was.

My first thought was that she was mine. She belonged to me exclusively. She was taller than I had expected, and boy, could she sing. I was completely thrilled with her and how talented she was. I almost felt as if I were the long-lost mother who had found her daughter. I felt instantly proud and instantly possessive.

That is my sister. I wanted to look around at all the audience members and say, "See that girl there, the pretty one, that's my sister. I know, she is beautiful, thank you. Yes, such talent, we are all so proud…."

At intermission, it was announced that the cast would be in the lobby to meet and greet and sign autographs for the children after the show.

My husband and I looked at each other in shock. She would be out there when we were leaving!

I panicked. What should I do? She didn't know I was there. I wasn't expecting her to see me or meet me. Should I leave now? Should we dash out at curtain call?

Should I stay and meet her?

We decided to stay, and the rest of the show was a blur.

We let the majority of the audience get out before us and allowed the crowds to settle down before joining them.

When we reached the lobby, I saw her right away. She was talking to a little girl who had loved the show and wanted her autograph. My sister was so sweet with the little girl, giving her a hug. Then she stood up and she saw me. The recognition was instant. She gasped and ran over and gave me the biggest hug. We were hugging and laughing. We pulled away and looked at each other closely.

"You're beautiful!" she exclaimed and pulled me back in for another hug.

She thought I was beautiful.

We were both overwhelmed and didn't know what to say. There was no time to really talk, and we were caught in an awkward moment of shock and excitement.

I was so sure that the first time I met her, I would cry, but there were no tears for either of us. My husband took our picture, and we said goodbye, leaving her to her audience and her well-deserved praise

I left, so appreciative for this amazing moment in my life and infatuated with the idea of having a sister. My sister. She was no longer just an email or a picture on Facebook. She was real, and she was happy to see me. The puzzle pieces were coming together nicely now. I was making real connections.

We are respecting privacy, so my 10 year old daughter drew a picture of the photo my husband snapped just before we left

"Look at this picture, baby, just look at us." I say holding out my iPhone to Rob, "can't you see how much we look alike?"

"Baby, I'm driving the car." He replies but still glances over.

"I'm still shaking," I admit, laughing. "I can't wait to show everybody."

"I'm really happy for you." He reaches across the car seat and touches my thigh, his hand warm and strong, like it always is.

"I still can't believe I didn't cry." I can't seem to stop talking about it.

"You guys were both so shocked," he paused. "I have to admit I teared up, I'm not gonna lie."

"You didn't!" I smacked his arm.

"Hey, I was surprised myself," he said, his macho side rearing its head, "but I was so happy for you. You waited so long for this, baby, and I was really glad we stayed."

I rested my head back on the car seat and watched the interstate fly past us, the setting sun sparkling through the trees and felt her hug the whole way home.

Later that night I couldn't help but think that I might have completely freaked her out by showing up unannounced. So, I gave her a quick call to explain, in my increasingly nervous and clumsy way that I wasn't actually a stalker or crazy person. We both got a good laugh out of it, her laughter, natural and palpable, wrapping me in it's softness.

She had called our mother to let her know and when she told her how I was even prettier in person our Mother started to cry.

She told me that no matter what had happened in their lives up to now, whether it was the passing of her grandparents, her father's illness, and even the divorce, nothing had made her mother cry more than talking about me. Deep down, that fulfilled me. In the oddest way, it made me think that there was hope, that she did love me deeply and would want to meet me someday.

The following spring, my sister came to Charleston for the weekend to stay with us and get to know us all better.

I was a nervous wreck. I wanted to make sure everything was perfect and that we'd have things to do and places to go. I wanted her to have a good time, and I wanted to make sure we had fun together. This was the most important moment in our relationship to date. I was having family, my family, my SISTER, come to visit.

She arrived on a Friday afternoon. My first thought, as she stepped out of the car was how nicely dressed she was for a road trip. *I would share this with Carol, my long-ago travel buddy as we lunched and discussed this important weekend. "Of course she did, Liz," Carol said over bites of Caesar salad, "She was coming to meet her sister."*

I prepared a meal at home so that we could be very casual and just spend the evening together with my husband and children. We opened champagne and toasted the occasion. We all had the best time staying up late playing games and laughing. The entire weekend was full of fun, and it was easy and comfortable. We even ended up hearing the same song over and over on the radio, every time we went somewhere, so we declared it our song. *We have a song, my sister and I.*

SOMEWHERE OUT THERE

I spent so many years thinking about my mother and wondering if she ever thought of me at all, or was I simply a bad memory discarded and forgotten.

When I was a freshman in college, the animated movie, *An American Tail*, was released. It was the story of a mouse separated from his family and his journey back to them. It had a song that climbed the billboard charts, "Somewhere Out There."

The song had me dissolving into a puddle of tears every time I heard it. I was never able to sing it the whole way through.

It spoke of wishing on the same star, even though they were separated and it rang in my heart like a lonely bell.

So that became my anthem and my wish. Are my mother and I looking at the same sky? Are there thoughts of me in her heart, too?

As I got to know my sister, I often asked questions about what kind of woman our mother was. What did they do together or what were their favorite things?

"Oh, we have a song." she said. "It's from *An American Tail*. Do you know it? It's a cartoon movie, the song, 'Somewhere Out There'?"

"Oh," I breathed out, speechless. I felt like I couldn't pull air into my lungs, and I was spinning. I saw stars in my eyes as the blood rushed from my head crashing into my feet and making me feel suddenly unsteady.

"Mom really loves that song." She was still talking. "We had the movie on videotape, and she rewound it over and over again and wrote down all the words. She was obsessed with it."

"But wait," I wanted to say, *"you can't have that song with her, that's my song with her. See, the mouse was separated from his mouse family, and he was singing that song to his mouse mother ABOUT his mouse mother, trying to connect. See, that's MY*

story, not yours. You got her. I did not get her. I AM THE SOMEONE OUT THERE!!"

Instead I said, "Yeah, I know that song very well. I used to think it was my song about finding her." I tried to laugh it off.

My sweet sister looked at me, with the same blue eyes as my mother, "Well, we can all share it now."

THE TIE THAT BINDS

When my sister left for home after our first weekend together, there was a true family connection, and we knew that this was going to be more than a casual relationship. The children filled the front door as she drove away, "Good bye Aunt ******* !!!" We had become a family.

I was walking on air. I practiced saying things like, "Oh, my sister and I do that." "Yes, well, my sister said…" "Oh, this? I got this from my sister!"

She ended up writing our mother a letter about her visit with us and left it under the mat of her front door one morning before work.

My sister's letter was full of love for me and my husband and children and steadfastly declared her decision that with or without her mother's involvement, she was now a proud Aunt and would be continuing on this journey to grow closer to her sister.

The dancer turned choreographer was delicately and elaborately staging the scene for the climactic number, which always closes Act I enticing the audience back for Act II.

You tell her Oprah.

It was this letter that finally got my mother's attention. My sister had the power that I could never possess, and my mother agreed to meet me.

I was forty-four. This was a moment I had wanted for the last twenty-nine years.

The day before I left I stopped by my adopted mother's house to tell her the news. I felt she should know too. She walked me to the door, like she always did and we said good bye. Then suddenly she reached out and hugged me.

"Good luck," she said into my long curly hair.

We are Butlers, and we are huggers.

We chose July 1. It was an extremely hot South Carolina day, and I wore a new pink dress that I had bought for the occasion. It seemed right to me that I was meeting my birth mother in a similar manner to meeting my own parents, pink dress and all, hot summer day ahead.

I had a long drive to get to my sister's house. So many thoughts were running around in my mind about what this moment would be like. I had waited a very long time. I was very emotional. I couldn't imagine a scenario where I didn't cry.

I didn't want to cry. That would ruin my perfectly applied makeup. I wanted to look good for her; I wanted to be pretty for her.

If I did cry, it would feel good to finally let it out. It would feel good to have my mother comfort me. Wipe away my tears. Hold me and say, "Shhh, sweetie, it's all going to be OK."

I was forty-four-years-old, a mother of four and I needed a Mommy.

I pulled into town just early enough to stop and use the ladies room and freshen up. Pulling into a chain restaurant, I got myself ready, taking a good long look in the mirror and quietly telling myself that it would be all right. The time was finally here.

On my way out, I decided to stop at the bar. One good shot would make this all a lot easier to tolerate.

"Sorry, ma'am, we don't serve liquor on Sundays."

Are you kidding me? You just have to make an exception. Do you realize what is happening to me today? What is wrong with you people? Where is your manager?

I found my way to my sister's house. A cute little neighborhood filled with young couples walking their dogs and a few small children toddling in small neat front yards. I parked and took a few deep breaths. I grabbed my phone and texted my husband.

The eagle has landed. Here goes nothin'.

I pulled down the car's rearview mirror and inspected my carefully applied makeup again.

I took a few deep breaths. I thought of my father.

"Do me a favor," he said, handing the check to me, "if you ever get to meet her, I want to get a chance to meet her, too.

DADDY

My phone rang at 5:00 a.m. I was instantly awakened, but my sleep-filled brain was confused. Was that my phone, or is my two-week-old son getting up for another feeding?

"Baby, get the phone," Rob said, his strong hand on my arm, "it must be the hospital."

I answered.

"Liz," my brother's tired voice came over the line, "It's me. I think it's about time. You need to come back."

I scrambled for my things. I thought to stop and mix some formula for the baby. My breasts had dried up already; so much stress, so much worry.

Dad had gone into the hospital over a month ago. His kidneys were infected, and they were not getting better with antibiotics. It was time to take more aggressive action.

Mom called me to tell me when the decision was made to check him into the hospital. Dad's mother had died of kidney failure. Mom told me that when Dad got off the phone with the doctor after learning he needed to go to the hospital, he sat on the edge of their neatly made bed and cried, afraid that he would go into the hospital and never come out.

He was eighty-three.

I never thought Daddy would not come home. He was so vibrant.

I called him every day from the hospital I was in after I had my son. This was the only birth of a child of mine that my Dad had missed. I know it made him sad.

We laughed that we were both in cheap threadbare gowns and how awful the food was.

At the end of every phone call, he would say, "Thank you for calling." That was code for "I love you," so I said, "Of course, Daddy, I love you, too."

As soon as I was able, I visited him in the hospital between baby feedings to cheer him up and take him pictures. He loved seeing his new grandson and would tear up.

"You'll see him very soon and get to hold him, Daddy." I'd kiss his bald head. I fed him pudding, the only thing he felt up to eating.

My brother and I spent a lot of time in that room, sending Mom home to get some rest while Dad napped. We sat mainly in silence or talking about easy things. Current events. Our children. If we had dared to talk about life with Dad, emotions would have run too high. We might be admitting that this was the end and neither of us were willing to be the first one to say it.

Mom and Dad had quit going to church years ago. They preferred to watch it on TV, but Dad still sent in his checks of support, so this got us a daily visit from the minister.

The minister stopped by one day when Jonathan and I were alone and, seeing Dad asleep, he just whispered some nice things to us about how the older gang at the church spoke so highly of Robert and what a great guy he was.

I remember my brother and I looking into each other's eyes at the same moment, trying not to laugh. Dad's name was John. The minister finally left, and we giggled like children as our father slept, dying slowly next to us.

I was alone with Dad the evening before the 5:00 a.m. phone call. I had a moment to sit there and talk to him. I wasn't sure if he could hear me. He was on a lot of morphine. He was sleeping on his side, but his hands were tightly gripping the bed rail, as if he were afraid to let go or he'd fall. Every so often, his eyes would fly open wildly and stare at me as if he didn't know who I was or where he was.

"Hey, Daddy," I would say, "I'm right here. It's OK to let go, Daddy. I understand if you have to go."

When he died, we were all there—Mom, Jonathan, his wife, my Aunt Elizabeth, and me. I was holding his hand when he took his final breath.

We stood there looking at him. He turned white so quickly. I thought it happened too fast. Couldn't I just have another minute?

My mother slowly stood up and tucked her pocketbook under her arms, the needlepoint she had been working on sticking carelessly out, threads hanging down the side, their bright colors in contrast to the gloom of the hospital room.

"Well, I guess we should go now," she said in the smallest of whispers.

Everyone else started to gather their things, but I didn't move. I just stared at Dad, watching him turn whiter before my eyes.

"Elizabeth," my mother was at the door holding it open, the bright lights from the hallway cutting through the darkness of the room, the noises from the nurses' station invading my grief. "It's time to go now." She looked old and tired from the tears we had all shed for this sweet man.

"She doesn't have to go yet," said the nurse, appearing in the doorway behind her, "That's her Daddy. Let her stay."

THE MEETING

I got out of the car at my sister's house in Rockville, carrying the love of my friends and husband and, as promised, the ghost of my Daddy along with me as I walked up to the door and knocked on it.

The door was flung wide open, and there she was. My mother. It was like looking into a mirror. Our matching blue eyes met. She held her arms out, and I fell into her warm embrace. I inhaled the scent of my mother's perfume—bright, floral. She smelled like spring. I wondered if she had always worn this scent. Is this what my mother always smelled like? I saw my sister standing behind us, so happy for us both in that moment. We were all laughing as tears sprang into our eyes.

"Let me look at you,"my mother said, holding me at arm's length. "Such a beautiful girl, my sweet daughter." Her hand caressed my face, and we hugged again.

"I've been such a fool to wait so long to meet you. I hope we can make up for lost time. I know you must have so many questions. Come in, come in. We have a lot of catching up to do. It's time you knew the entire story, isn't it, my darling girl?"

That was what I was hoping for. However, it didn't exactly happen that way.

Our meeting was calm and refined. It was more like I had walked into a cocktail party with some of the nicest people I had ever met. We were all sincerely interested in each other, but there were clear boundaries, and feelings were held in tight check. We were all on our best behavior.

It was hard for me not to stare at my beautiful mother. I knew one thing right away. I loved her. I loved the way she brushed her hair off her face, just like I do. The way she wrinkled her nose when she laughed. I do that, too.

I asked for a picture before I left, and we stood together in front of my sister's fireplace mantle. My mother leaned her head next to mine and held onto me with both hands. It was the closest we would come to being emotional.

I loved looking at that picture. I shared it with all of my friends, and we marveled over the similarities.

This moment reminded of a time when my oldest daughter, Daphne, was not quite two-years-old. We were getting ready for her bedtime. It was my favorite time to be with her, when it was quiet and we were snuggled on her bed, reading books and sharing stories from the day.

We sat in silence for a moment on this particular night. I twirled one of her long, red curls around my finger and said, "Daphne, do you remember what God looks like?"

She turned to look at me, placed her little soft hand on my face, and said, "Like you," she paused so briefly, "and like me. Like you and me."

Now, looking at this photo of my mother and me, I suddenly understand the brilliance of the innocent little thing Daphne said. God is love. We are love. When we look at each other, we can see it in its purest form.

LIZ NOIR: JANET BABY CASE: CASE CLOSED

So there is my story told again.

Throughout the process of getting all of it out of my head and onto paper, the thought occurred to me that this was more than a story about me searching for my birth mother. It is a story about mothers—the mother who had me and the mother who raised me.

When I think about my birth mother, I marvel at the strides she has taken to allow me into her life—from vehement denial through reluctant admittance and, finally, exuberant acceptance.

I often wonder if I am just putting myself in the same situation with a different family, locking myself into a lifelong struggle for acknowledgement. The insecurities and doubts I have always grappled with are never far from my mind. I get jealous of my birth mother's love for her other children the same way I was always jealous of Jonathan. I tell myself it's different this time, she only needs time to get used to me being in her life, but isn't that how I think of my adoptive mother, too? One day she will come around and we will bond? One day I will feel like Jonathan. I will be the favorite.

I see so many similarities in looks and talents between my sister and me, and I think that my birth mother really got lucky. She had to give away her first daughter, but she still got the chance to raise "me." I will never know how it would have been to have a mother like her.

When I think about my adoptive mother now, I think the opportunity for the greatest love and friendship was lost to both of us. Here we were, two children who never knew their real mothers, raised by other women. Right there, we should have had a bond, an opportunity to show that it didn't matter who gave birth to you. It was OK to feel different. *We accept you for just who you are. You are safe here.*

I always thought I needed a mother who thought I was special and unique and loved me unconditionally because of that. My birth mother was able to fill that void, to pump extra air into the sagging balloon edges of my heart. She did it so immediately and effortlessly and made sure I knew it and felt it. Because of that gift I am able to love the mother who raised me with far less complications. I can now love her for who she is, not what I need her to give me.

I used to look for a mother's love in so many different places. The men in my life, even my own children, but they could never do it. Husbands love passionately and children love selfishly. I can stop looking, my heart is calmer now.

I see my adoptive mother now in her old age and how her attachment to her things is so important to her. *Who will take care of my furniture and my things after I'm gone? What will become of them?* I now understand this. I understand her need to hold on to something concrete.

Children grow up and move away. They never call or visit often enough. Husbands die. She is left with her things. If she regrets keeping a wall up in our relationship, I don't see it. She still does not talk about her feelings. If I ever thought to bring it up, she would tell me I was ridiculous. She would say she never acted the way I remember and everything was fine. Subject closed.

She said to me once, "I did the best I could." I believe her. In the fractured way that she knows love, she loves me very deeply and I love her, too.

She told me that she felt like the villain in my life story, that she wasn't good enough. I told her that maybe neither of us were good enough, but we still have time. I will never leave her side. I will take her to her doctor's appointments. I will run to any Bi-Lo. I will bring flowers for her garden. She was there for me in the best way she knew to be and I will give her my best too. She is my mother and I will guide her through the rest of the days of our lives together her hand in mine.

Well, anyway.

Then there is the mother that I am. This story cannot be written yet. I am still raising my children, doing my best with the feelings I have, making my own mistakes, fueling their life stories. What will they tell their children about me? How will I be remembered?

Will they call or visit often enough?

I did the best I could.

EPILOGUE

******* Baby Case

Evaluation

03/18/16: Elizabeth seems to be functioning very well with her biological family. She and her mother, ******, are getting closer every day, and they have found great happiness in each other's company. What was once rather formal and polite has grown into genuine love and devotion. The biological siblings have bonded and are continuing to cultivate their relationships. Her biological sister, *******, celebrated her wedding last year, and Elizabeth was in attendance with her husband and four beautiful children. Her biological brother, ***, has moved to **********, but they still communicate frequently and have formed a great friendship. Her children refer to him as THE Uncle.

****** has not disclosed the name of Elizabeth's birth father to her, and Elizabeth's contentment leaves her unwilling to upset the applecart. She is respecting ******'s decision, despite new clues that have tempted Liz Noir: Girl Detective. Elizabeth's adoptive mother is still very much in Elizabeth's life, although her Parkinson's disease greatly limits her involvement. She refers to Elizabeth's biological family as "your people." This shows great progress from the sullen silence that has been her previous response to all adoptive information. She seems to be handling the situation well and adjusting as any adoptive mother possibly could.

It is with great joy that I can report that on Elizabeth's most recent leap year birthday celebration, her biological mother spent it with

her, and for the first time in forty-eight years
(twelve, if you are counting in leap years),
these two were together to celebrate.

It appears this placement is going well.

ACKNOWLEDGEMENTS

First and foremost I have to thank Brian Turner for refusing to be my ghost writer and sending me on this journey of exploration and release.

I am so glad I know Jessica Hoefer. She was a patient and thoughtful editor of this book and I could not have done it without her help, guidance and enthusiasm for my story.

Diane Anderson helped me see this book with the eyes of an adopted mother and her help was instrumental as well.

Thank you to Shelly Little for being a thoughtful reader of this book and for being a mother to D'ondra.

Keely Enright, you put a lot of time into reading this and helping me psychoanalyze myself. You should charge by the hour.

And to my last and final, hunky husband, Rob, and my four children who had to hear the words "the book" seventy gazillion times and never once rolled their eyes. I love you, freaks.

ABOUT THE AUTHOR

Seriously? You need to know more?

THE THREE R'S OF 21ST CENTURY READING

- **Read** the book - Authors love to sell books, but they really want buyers to read them. If you've come this far, thank you again for reading. Your investment of time matters to me.
- **Review** the book - Amazon and Goodreads don't tabulate book rankings based on sales alone. Reviews weigh heavily into the algorithms for book rankings. Your review matters. More reviews mean higher rankings, more impressions and ultimately, more readers. Please take five minutes and write a review of this book. If you write the review on Goodreads first, you can copy and paste it into Amazon.
- **Recommend** the book - The people in your life value your opinion. If you enjoyed this book, recommend it to five people. Over lunch or coffee. At the water cooler. On the sidelines. Let people see and hear your enthusiasm for this story. Some of them will thank you for showing them the way to a good book.

CPSIA information can be obtained
at www.ICGtesting.com
Printed in the USA
LVHW04s2332250718
584995LV00001B/156/P